WYMONDHAM P.

IN THE E*

SIXTEENTH CENTURY

BRENDA GARRARD

Brenda Garrard

Illustrations by Anne Hoare

Cover Illustration: The fraternity of Our Lady's Light made a "gathering" or collection in the town as part of their procession.

Copies may be obtained from Wymondham Heritage Museum,
The Bridewell, Wymondham, Norfolk, NR18 0NS

ISBN   0 900616 68 7

Printed and published by Geo. R. Reeve Ltd.,
9-11 Town Green, Wymondham, Norfolk, NR18 0BD.

2

CONTENTS

Nomina fratrum et sororum Gilde Omnium Sanctorum Anno Dñi
Millesimo CCCC⁰ secundo Et Anno Regni Regis Henrici
Septimi decimo octavo

Magister Robert Gyby vicary	John Dalby e cō) ens
Richard Denton e cō) ens	James Shopsede e cō ens
Robert Rolland e cō) ens	Thomē Walton e cō) ens
william Blythe e cō) ens	Richarde Deynes e cō) ens
Gregory Denton	Thomē Spony e cō) ens
willm Payn	Thomē Bedell e
Richarde Payn e cō) ens	James Petyt e cō) ens
John Denthorp e cō) ens	Thomē Jeffson e cō) ens
John Anson e cō) ens	Thomē Dobbes
Petyr Stanton e cō) ens	Thomē Dobsynt e cō) ens
Harry Seman e cō) ens	Richarde Parson e cō) ens
willm Parke e cō) ens	Harry Brotton
willm Fenge e cō) ens	Jean aj arara secundo
willm Tresshels e cō) ens	willm Ffodymont e cō) ens
willm Robalds e cō) ens	John Typ e cō) ens
willm Workman	willm Dalbis
willm Rolland e cō) ens	Edmunde aj dymyj
Agnes Rolland wedewe	Je dñj aj witt in
John Dalbir e cō) ens	Richland Anson
Edmund Fawell alia Robyn	Anno Dñi gillino iiij
willm Smyth	Dionise Jawbus Anson
Margaret Hynde	Margaretta Denton
John Shotenden e cō) ens	Margaretta Dobbys
Robert Dalby et cō) ens	Alice myttre
Thomē Bedfor e cō) ens	Je dñj gillino lxxxx ō
Thomē Blythe e cō) ens	willm Dalbis
Gregory Dalbow e cō) ens	Thomē Tayow
Richarde Wyhtow e cō) ens	Dompnus Thomē ingesim
Thomē Foster	Dompnus willm brys
Ser Thomē Dalbe	Robert Jon myndowrtoj ō

FOREWORD

This study is the result of ten years of research, fitted into a very busy schedule. Canon Martin Smith was right when he described it as a labour of love. It is not intended to be an academic evaluation of the gilds, but an attempt to get behind their operations and discover something of the lives of the Wymondham people of the early sixteenth century who were affected by them.

This was made possible in the first place by the advice and encouragement of the pioneer tutors of the M.A. course in Local and Regional History at U.E.A., Professor A. Hassell Smith and Dr. Victor Morgan. It was Hassell who introduced me to the transcription of medieval and early modern manuscripts.

Thanks are also due to Paul Cattermole, honorary archivist at Wymondham Abbey, Janet Smith, Wymondham town archivist, Barbara Green, honorary librarian of the Norfolk and Norwich Archaeological Society, Canon Martin Smith, Father John Barnes, John Wilson, and the staff of the Norfolk Record Office and the UEA Library.

I am particularly grateful to Anne Hoare for agreeing to do the illustrations and helping with the location of gild halls, Roger for his tolerance, proof reading and encouragement, and Sara for her enthusiastic and invaluable help with the cross-referencing.

Brenda Garrard

Wymondham 2003

Opposite – A page from the account book of the Gild of All Saints listing members in 1502

WYMONDHAM PARISH GILDS IN THE EARLY SIXTEENTH CENTURY

INTRODUCTION

Life in medieval England could be extremely hard, and the survival of the individual often depended upon the support of others. This was just as true in Wymondham as in all the rural areas of England. Support, and co-operation within the community, was essential at all times of the year in the medieval "open-field" system of agriculture, but it was crucial at the key times of ploughing, sowing and harvesting the small, individual strips of land. As well as the obvious practical benefits from this arrangement, it generated a strong sense of identity and social cohesion within the community, and this cohesion naturally spread to religion, which permeated every aspect of medieval life. The ideal of a Christian brotherhood with a common purpose became very attractive to inhabitants of both town and country, and it led to the initial establishment of gilds, fraternities and brotherhoods, which were attached to the parish church.

These religious gilds are often confused with the more well-known craft gilds responsible for the organisation and regulation of a particular craft, which in addition helped their members in times of hardship and sickness. They were, by their very nature, somewhat limited in their appeal and membership, and were more common in the towns and larger communities. In this case, the craft itself was the bond of unity between the members.

What was the common bond in the religious gilds? It is difficult to answer this question without reference to the belief in purgatory which had developed during the twelfth century, and was central to religious thinking up to the Reformation. It was thought that after death the souls of those who had led an exemplary life on earth obtained immediate access to the place of happiness or heaven, while those of the wicked were straightway sent to hell. The vast majority of the dying, however, fell between these two extremes, those who were saved but did not merit direct admission to the heavenly realm. These souls were sent to purgatory and remained there for as long as their lives on earth merited, before they too were allowed into heaven. To ensure that purgatory was not seen as a soft option for the increasing numbers of potential inhabitants, it had to be depicted as a place to be feared, and this is why medieval writing and painting tended to emphasise the horrific sufferings inflicted there by devils.

The natural response of the living to this was to consider ways in which wayward souls could be helped during their sojourn in purgatory, and how the time spent there could be minimised. The remedies ranged from founding a monastery to the lighting of a candle before the image of a saint in the parish church, or the gift of a penny to a beggar. The most popular method adopted by the wealthy was the endowment of intercessory masses or chantries to be celebrated by priests on behalf of departed souls, for a period of time, perhaps for several decades or even in perpetuity. For the poorer majority, however, such a legacy was impossible, but the membership of a gild was a very satisfactory alternative. Services of prayers and masses for the dead were the central features of the activities of a gild or fraternity, and there was always at least one annual requiem for the dead brethren. Members of gilds would have been comforted by the knowledge that their funeral service would be attended by their friends, who, according to gild rules, would be fined for non-attendance at such an event. Moreover their bodies would be escorted back to the parish with full ceremony if they died within a radius of five miles.

Although religion may have been the main reason for the formation of the gilds, other benefits emerged for those belonging to them. Patricia Basing, editing the book, "Parish Fraternity Register", suggests that the social and economic aspects of gild membership cannot be ignored, and were at the very heart of a gild's existence. For friends who lived near each other, the gild provided an ideal focus for social activity and support, at a time when there were very few opportunities to escape the daily grind of manual labour and the harsh reality of early sixteenth century life. Common economic interest also drew people together, and some gilds encouraged enterprise and even provided members with the opportunity to borrow money or stock, to help them in times of expansion or crisis, before the provision of banks or borrowing facilities for the common man.

For these reasons and others, gild membership became very

attractive and many were established throughout the country. In rural Norfolk they seemed to have been particularly popular. Although East Anglia lay outside the area of fifteenth century warfare, life in the region was still very insecure, and religion offered calm and stability in day - to – day existence. In 1389 Richard ll's Parliament had instructed all religious gilds to send in a return, describing their foundation and form of government, oaths of entry, meetings and feasts, liberties and customs, together with a list of all their property, whether in the form of land, houses or goods. The purpose behind this request is unclear, and no reasons were given at the time. Suggestions made since have included the costs of war and the king's extravagance, their potential value for tax or confiscation, and even the possibility of the gilds being a source of seditious activities. Norfolk heads the list of counties at this time, with a total of 164 gilds, but the only Wymondham gild to be included in the return is the one dedicated to St. Thomas. Many more were formed during the next hundred years, assuming that the practice in Wymondham was repeated throughout the county.

Parish gilds were always dedicated to a particular patron or patrons, who could be called upon to petition for the souls of gild members awaiting their release from purgatory. The most popular patron was the Virgin Mary, chosen by about a quarter of all gilds, who was closely followed by St. Peter, All Saints and the Holy Trinity. While it is quite easy to see why these three were popular, it is more difficult to account for the number of dedications to St. John the Baptist. Perhaps the answer lies in the date of his feast day, June 24th, which coincides with Midsummer Day, an ideal time for celebration and merriment. Another decisive factor in the dedication of a gild was the extent to which the patron could be depicted in pageants and processions. St. George and the dragon were ideal for this and offered much scope for theatricals.

What was the parish of Wymondham like at the beginning of the sixteenth century? We know that it was the second largest in the county, and of sufficient size to merit the appointment of four churchwardens instead of the customary two. Part of the wood-pasture region of the county, its heavy clay soils were better for rearing cattle than sheep, and did little to encourage arable farming, although mixed crops were grown. John Pound's map of the distribution of wealth in Norfolk in the early sixteenth century, based on the subsidy returns and military surveys for the 1520s, puts the parish of Wymondham in the third highest quadrant of the wealthy regions. This was, no doubt, an important factor in the growth of religious gilds within the parish. At the time of their dissolution, there appear to have been twelve gilds operating in Wymondham, although this figure is open to question. The naming of them followed the national pattern, and they were dedicated to:-

All Saints*
Corpus Christi
Our Lady's Light*
St. George
St. John the Baptist*
St. Margaret
St. Peter
St. Thomas the Martyr
The Holy Cross
The Holy Trinity (sometimes called the Spooner Row Gild)*
The Nativity of the Blessed Virgin Mary*

* Account Book in Abbey muniment room

There is considerable doubt about the existence of a gild dedicated to St. Andrew, and I have found only one reference to St. Andrew in the wills of the period. In 1510, Thomas Dalys, a priest, left 2s for repairs to the "high altar of St. Andrew of Wymondham". He does not mention the word "gild" in this bequest, but specifically refers to the gilds of St. Thomas, Our Lady, and All Saints in others. On the other hand, Martin Jarvis, Vicar of Wymondham, writing in a guide book to Wymondham Abbey in 1914, supports the idea that one existed. He quotes from a document in the muniment room: "The Gild of St. Andrew erected a rode-loft at their altar in the church in 1497." This appears to be an exact copy of Blomefield's comments in 1805, and we know that Blomefield's list of gilds is inaccurate. Since he omits Corpus Christi and considers those dedicated to our Lady's Light and the Nativity of the Blessed Virgin Mary as a single entity, we cannot rely on his evidence alone in this matter, and I have not included the gild of St. Andrew in my list. The population of Wymondham in the early sixteenth century was approximately 2,000 and it is obvious that they, together with the parishioners who lived outside the town and those from neighbouring parishes, had plenty of choice of which particular gilds they wished to join. And join they certainly did.

Tragically, for both the town and local historians, many valuable records and documents relating to the Wymondham gilds have disappeared over the centuries. It is certain that some nineteenth century antiquarians are partly responsible for this loss. On his own admission, solicitor G. A. Carthew, writing in 1884, admitted to removing some account books from the parish chest in order to copy them. He obviously found the task too daunting to complete, and returned them, or rather, thought he had returned them. His somewhat cavalier attitude to such valuable documents is illustrated by his own comment: "It appears however that I neglected to return a parcel of loose, unbound papers, part of the same collection, which turned up the other day".

We are fortunate that he did publish a few of his transcriptions in full and summaries of others in the "Norfolk Archaeology" series, before losing the originals. Today, the only records we have in the muniment room in the Abbey are the account books for the five gilds dedicated to All Saints, Our Lady's Light, St John the Baptist, the Holy Trinity, and the Nativity of the Blessed Virgin Mary. The loss of documentation relating to the Gild of St. Thomas the Martyr is particularly disappointing both from a regional and national point of view, since it was one of the earliest dedicated to this saint in the whole country. Thomas à Becket was canonised in 1173, and the Wymondham gild was founded in 1187, two years before the death of King Henry ll.

Thomas à Becket's Chapel used by the gild drawn in 1869
(Wymondham Library Records)

Other helpful sources of information regarding the activities of gilds, which are still in the muniment room in the abbey, are the bede roll of 1524, together with many title deeds from the years 1225 to 1546, and several single documents, mostly relating to the transaction of land, and church inventories.

Elsewhere, the wills of the period, i.e. 1499-1546, proved in the Archdeaconry Court of Norfolk or the Norwich Consistory Court, add to our knowledge, since they not only disclose bequests to the gilds, but also provide additional facts on gild properties and activities. It was not unusual to leave money for religious purposes at this time, and practically all the Wymondham testators began their wills by leaving small sums to the parish church, "for tithes and offerings forgotten", or for specific repairs. Most also left small sums to the cathedral church in Norwich and the "lazars without the gates" of the city. In addition, of the 167 Wymondham wills studied, more than half (89) included a bequest to at least one gild, some to as many as five or six.

Burial practices in sixteenth century England were somewhat crude by today's standards. For extra fees it was possible to be interred within the church itself, but very shallow graves were dug, and the uncoffined, shrouded bodies were often disturbed by new arrivals. Nevertheless, in Wymondham, such a request was sometimes made, usually by the more prosperous parishioners. It is interesting to note that in 1537 vicar John Drye arranged for his burial place to be "where his friends wished". It was the responsibility of the gilds to ensure that their members were buried with due reverence and respect, and they would pay the expenses if the deceased had left insufficient money to do so. Individual gilds had their own rules, but all required members to attend the funeral obits held in the parish church.

This was not the only occasion when the members met together. They also assembled in happier times. Perhaps the most enjoyable of these was when the annual feast was celebrated, usually in the gild's own hall. The outlay for it was sometimes met from the gild funds, but more often, was paid for by the members themselves. What was certain is that the members enjoyed a welcomed, if rare, break from the monotony of everyday life, and they could well be forgiven if the consumption of ale occasionally got out of hand. The requisite dirge for departed souls and requiem mass on the following day meant that the brethren were forced to return to normality very quickly.

Early gilds were organised along democratic lines. There was usually one leader, the alderman, who was chosen by a group of twelve men, referred to as the Election, and who were appointed themselves by the main body of members. The number twelve had special significance, and was chosen to parallel the number of disciples of Jesus. The alderman was usually a priest or a person of some wealth or importance within the town. His duties were quite onerous; he checked the attendance at all functions, ensured that gild rules were kept and authorised the leasing of lands. Most important of all was his oversight of the gild's financial affairs, and his ability to supplement any shortfall of funds for as long as necessary. At other times his authority was restricted, and he needed the backing of the elected twelve to seal official gild documents. If his performance in the post was unsatisfactory, gild members possessed the ultimate sanction, since the election of the alderman was an annual event.

Membership of a gild was open to all who wished to join, irrespective of sex or social status. It was also possible to join after death by writing such a request and the required donation in one's will, but in Wymondham only one person seems to have taken advantage of this opportunity. Wives joined at the same time as their husbands or followed a year or two later to spread the cost of the entry fee which was about 12d per person, although some gilds offered a "cut rate" of 20d for husband and wife. In spite of the rather rigid divisions of society found in the Middle Ages, it was not uncommon for master and servant to belong to the same gild, but with only one exception, to which we shall refer later, no woman held any office. The initiation ceremony on joining involved the swearing of an oath of allegiance, in the presence of the alderman, with the right hand on a wax candle. Loyalty was, however, not to the officers, but to the gild itself.

We have seen that there were financial benefits to the individual of belonging to a gild: funeral costs would be met if the individual had insufficient funds, and grants would be made during a member's life if he or she fell on hard times. On the other hand, the gild itself profited from the experience of its members in dealing with financial affairs. Indeed, before the 1530s it was this successful management of finance which was to become one of the causes of the gilds' ultimate downfall. They simply became too prosperous. After his successful despoliation of the monasteries in 1536 and 1539, Henry Vlll found them easy prey when he needed further financial support for his wars with France. Parliament was therefore persuaded to pass the necessary legislation to ban the provision of lights before images and to close the chantries and private chapels.

In most cases this wealth had been accumulated gradually, the result of shrewd investments and careful management of funds, rather than by large endowments and legacies. This was certainly true in Wymondham. Most gilds owned a gildhall at some time, where they met to celebrate the annual feast and hold their drinkings. These were nothing like the elaborate halls of the craft gilds found in London today, but very simple buildings, roughly constructed of timber and wattle and daub, with a thatched roof. Most gilds had acquired other properties by the beginning of the sixteenth century, and the rents of lands and properties figure prominently in the gild accounts. Some of these were owned entirely by the gilds themselves, but others were rented from manors and re-let at a profit. Tenements, barns and animals, particularly cows in Wymondham, were also rented out to individuals on a yearly basis, and for some it offered them their first experience of animal husbandry.

As for the gild halls themselves, there are few clues today to their exact whereabouts, and I am most grateful to Anne Hoare for helping me to establish some possible locations. Where we have been successful in linking a property or an area to a particular gild, the halls will be discussed in the sections on them. Others, which are less certain, are briefly mentioned here.

There is definite evidence of a gild property in Vicar Street. In the Wymondham Town Book 1663-1671, John Crow is shown as the occupier of "the guildhouse yard with part of a house thereupon built in Town Green". Further evidence is found in an attachment to an abstract of title, of approximately 1740, in the form of a plan, which shows a property in Vicar Street marked "supposed town lands called Guild Yard". Next to this are shown Canham's shop, house and yard.

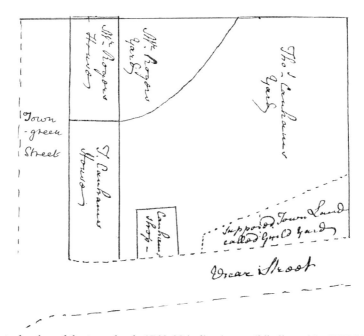

Part of a plan of the town lands 1768-88 indicating a gildhall yard In 1768 Mary Canham was admitted to a toft or tenement in Middleton on the death of her father John Crow, thereby linking the two references to the same property.
(Wymondham Town Archive)

Another document in the Wymondham town archive, "An Abridgement of the Lands of the Queen's Manor 1769", describes the position of one property as "being in Vicar Street, that is to say between the guildhall in part......" Other evidence, this time by word of mouth, comes from the present owner of Rook House, Number 8 Vicar Street, who was told by her solicitor that her house had been a gild hall, and a cottage in her garden had been used for storing gild banners. After an exhaustive study we have been unable to place the hall exactly in relation to the road, although the most likely site is where Number 8 now stands. Evidence from reports of the 1615 Fire in Wymondham refers to a gild hall being rebuilt for the use of the town, which is thought to be the Number 8 we see today. In fact, it was rented out rather than used by the town officials, who preferred instead to meet at the school house in Middleton Street.

The Vicar Street site described as gild house yard as it is today

A possible site for the gild hall in Vicar Street. In Wymondham gild yards could be on the opposite side of the road to the gild hall. Vicar Street had cottages where the war memorial now stands and the alignment of the street may have been somewhat different

Further along Town Green and just into Cock Street, another gild hall may be indicated by a map of the town lands of Wymondham made in 1822.

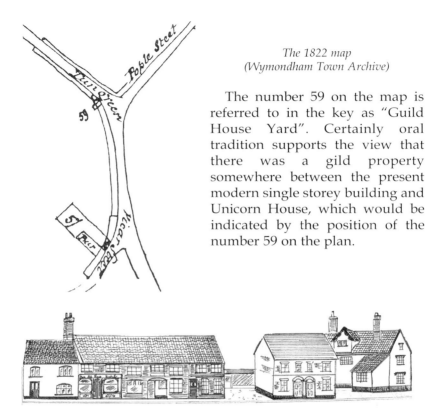

The 1822 map
(Wymondham Town Archive)

The number 59 on the map is referred to in the key as "Guild House Yard". Certainly oral tradition supports the view that there was a gild property somewhere between the present modern single storey building and Unicorn House, which would be indicated by the position of the number 59 on the plan.

Properties in the area of "number 59, Gild House Yard" today. Local tradition has it that there was a gild hall now demolished on the site of the present "modern" shop, which was also the site of petrol pumps

One or two other buildings in the town have traditionally been considered to have been gild halls, but we have no definite proof of these.

Loans, subject to a flat rate of 10% interest per annum, were made available to members, many of whom made use of this facility if they could find a friend who was prepared to act as surety for them. The gild account books which still remain give lists of their stockholders, together with the progress of the interest payments and the repayments of the loans, and they reveal interesting details of the financial state of some of the individuals involved. Other important sources of income for the Wymondham gilds were the annual drinkings, admission or ingress fees, and the collections or "gatherings" made at special events.

But it was not all profit, and, as one would expect, expenses were incurred. Substantial repairs were constantly having to be made to gild properties and were sometimes necessary to the patron's "chapel" or altar within the parish church. Gild priests had to be paid for their services, and the supply of wax for torches and candles always needed to be replenished. Candles used for masses had to be of pure wax, but those used for funeral services could be of inferior yellow wax. Tallow candles were only used for illumination. Torches were a coarse form of taper and used to escort the deceased to their funerals. Large tapers, called serges, were placed by the body while it was still within the church. In addition to these expenses, money was sometimes given to relieve members, particularly widows, who had fallen on hard times, a practical expression of the brotherly love and solidarity at the core of the ideology of the gild, and which must have been a great comfort to the beneficiaries. Small donations to local lazar houses and the general poor of the town were also a regular feature in gilds' accounts.

In the larger communities, gilds were very prosperous and some to such an extent that they became practically the main body of parishioners. Following the gift of a Royal Charter by Henry V in 1417, for unknown reasons, apart from the fact that he was the king's favourite saint, the gild of St. George in Norwich became a perpetual community with royal protection, and liberties and franchises enjoyed by corporate bodies in the country. Whilst retaining its religious and charitable character, this gild became a body with a written constitution, which was of particular significance when the 1547 Act of Parliament abolished all fraternities and gilds throughout the country. The gild of St. George in Norwich, with its written charter and safeguards, was able to continue, and merged with the ruling body of the city, enabling it to play an integral part in local government.

Religious gilds in other towns and cities were not as fortunate as this. By the middle of Henry Vlll's reign, their nature had started to change, and many began to lose something of their democratic character. Poorer people were discouraged from joining, and holding office in a gild began to be associated with status and social prestige. Other changes were taking place in the country generally, and the spread of the Reformation, with its new doctrines and ideas, resulted in less dependency on the old.

The Reformation had begun with Martin Luther's attack on indulgences. His doctrine of salvation by faith alone dealt a lethal blow to the belief in purgatory among his followers, and in 1530 he "declared war" on the doctrine. In England, Henry Vlll followed the progress of the reformation in Europe with interest. Most people would say that he adapted and adopted it to suit his own purposes. For whatever reason, in the "King's Book" of 1543, he prohibited the use of the term "purgatory" and made no reference to the continued sufferings of the dead. The "new" religion gave individuals direct access to their Maker via Christ, and they were therefore able to pray for themselves.

Gilds were now forced to change their ideals and practices, but it was their wealth which proved to be one of the final causes of their demise. The smaller monasteries had been dissolved in 1536 and the larger ones three years later. For a time the king was solvent, but by 1545 he had spent or given away much of the proceeds from the monasteries, and needed further revenues to fund his wars with Scotland and France. He complained that the gilds were no longer functioning "to virtuous and godly purposes". By an act of parliament that year, all the properties of the 2,374 gilds, chantries, free chapels and fraternities were granted to the crown. A further Act, passed by the first parliament of Edward VI's reign, explicitly condemned the doctrine of purgatory and empowered the government to seize any remaining capital devoted to the support of prayers for the dead. The promise that such funds would be used for the foundation of schools was partially kept in Wymondham, where the former chapel of St. Thomas was converted into a school and endowed with some of the lands once belonging to the gilds. However this was not the first "school" to exist within the town. In the accounts of the gild of the Nativity of the Blessed Virgin Mary for 1504 William Irby is described as a schoolmaster, and the churchwardens' accounts for 1544-1546 record payments to another unnamed schoolmaster, to Adam Bale for repairing the school house, and to William Ryngwood for setting up stools there.

The former chapel of St. Thomas à Becket as a school in 1903
(Wymondham Library Records)

Before this, however, enthusiasm for the gilds in the town had already begun to wane. The account books reveal that the scale of activity, together with the number of members, had been decreasing gradually for some time. It would appear that the community of Wymondham was well-aware of the religious changes taking place throughout the country, and, by the time of the 1545 Act, several gilds had already disposed of their possessions, to the benefit of the funds of the parish church. However, there is evidence to suggest that one or two were still meeting in the town as late as 1548.

In the following chapters, the gilds for which we still have full accounts are studied in detail. Of necessity, those for whom little documentation is available must be considered more briefly. Christian names have been modernised, but surnames appear as in the original documents, sometimes resulting in two or more different spellings. Sums of money are in the units of the early sixteenth century, i.e. pounds(£), shillings(s), and pence(d), or marks.

THE GILD OF THE NATIVITY OF THE BLESSED VIRGIN MARY

The monogram traditionally known as the consecration stone on the second pillar from the west in the north aisle of Wymondham Abbey. The name Maria is in a cipher with a crown above it and the letters M and T laid out in dressed flints the wrong way round

One of the more popular gilds in Wymondham at this time was that dedicated to the Nativity of the Blessed Virgin Mary. It had been formed in 1415 by a group of seven men:- Richard Knight, Robert Bird, Adam Joby, William Barker, Thomas Cowper, William Skinner and Clement Master, for the purpose of "honouring and worshipping the Virgin Mary." The founders also hoped that she would pray for them, and intercede on their behalf to ensure that their souls spent the minimum amount of time in purgatory.

The documentation for this gild is good. There is the original hand-written list of gild regulations and the account book for the years 1458 to 1544, both of which are still in the muniment room of the Abbey. The list, compiled by the founding members in 1415, was written at a later date, probably by one of the monks in the Abbey, since both the paper used and the style and handwriting are considerably superior to those of the account book. The only set of Wymondham gild rules still in existence, it is extremely important in that it gives us a clear description of the aims and objectives of this gild, which appear to be very similar to those of the others. Other very useful documents are two lists of new entrants to the gild. The first was begun in 1475 with annual additions for each year up to 1508. The second, based on the first starts with the year 1498 but was written in 1509 when a cost of 4d is recorded in the main accounts for that year, " to the gild book papyr and wrytyng newe a register of the namys of the brothers and sisters."

The focal point of the religious activity of the gild was the chapel in the north aisle of the Abbey, dedicated to the Virgin Mary. An image of the Virgin stood on the special altar, in front of which was a candle, maintained at the expense of the gild.

The lady chapel is at the east end of the north aisle. In earlier times the aisle was much narrower

Two members, or "guardians of the light", were appointed annually to purchase the necessary wax and ensure that the candle continued to burn. Constant references to the purchase of this wax appear in the gild account book, which was a regular drain on the funds. Gifts were often made by the brethren to furnish their chapel, and some remembered the Gild of the Blessed Virgin Mary when making their wills. Evidence for this can be found in the Bede Roll of 1524, as well as from surviving wills. Before he died in 1500, Robert Chapelyn and his wife Christian donated a tabernacle for the image of the Virgin. Robert had been a man of some substance and position in the town, and left many bequests to his family and the church. In addition to his earlier generosity to the gild, he made further provision in his will, with the gift of a close, sometimes referred to as Odards Close and at other times as the "Wooded Close". At one time, this close may well have belonged to Odard of Snettisham, who presented it to the monastery, together with other lands in Wicklewood, in the thirteenth century. Robert was a member of several gilds and his will makes interesting reading. In addition to bequests to the gilds of the Holy Trinity, St. Thomas and St. Margaret, the Abbey and convent were left 40s "when they do fetche home ther lytyll bell and do hang it up". They were also left his windmill if they "vexe not nor trouble not myn executors", a condition which perhaps reveals a certain frustration that Robert must have experienced in his dealings with Abbot John Kyrtelyng and his monks in the past. Other donations to the church made by gild members included an image of Our Lady provided by John Daundy and a red vestment, two mass books and a grail given by priest Thomas Plomer.

One of the most important of the gild rules was that all members should be at the parish church of Wymondham on the Sunday after the feast of the Nativity of the Blessed Virgin (September 8th) if they dwelt within 40 miles of it, unless prevented by sickness. They were to process, with their candles and banners, to a Mass dedicated to the worship of "our lady who is Queen of Heaven".

The Gild of the Nativity of the Blessed Virgin Mary processing to Mass

Gild members failing to attend were fined, usually a sum equivalent to the cost of four pounds of wax. At some point during this annual gild Mass, an offertory was taken for distribution among the needy. It had also been agreed at the gild's foundation that all members should meet on the Sunday before the feast of St. John the Baptist at Midsummer and take confession "in the best manner". Attendance was also compulsory at any special profit-making occasion, usually a drinking, organised to enhance gild funds. This was carefully monitored by the alderman and the beadle, and those failing to turn up without a good reason were fined two pounds of wax, as Harry Seman found to his cost in 1503.

The officers of the Gild of the Blessed Virgin Mary fitted the usual pattern of gilds at this time. The most important position was that of alderman, the election for whom was held on the Sunday following the feast of St. Luke (October 18th), when the twelve special members, the Election, made their choice. This was a particularly important day, and all members were required to take any gildstock they had borrowed "on the pain of double its value", and pay the interest due on it. The rules decreed that once chosen, an alderman should be re-elected, unless he was prevented by illness. For his part, the alderman, having once accepted the position, could not relinquish it without paying a fine of three pounds of wax. The list of aldermen below confirms that this gild observed the two rules as far as possible, thereby creating a stability of leadership from which all members would benefit. William Chapelyn was forced to take over as alderman and make the account for the year 1500 "pro patre" on the illness of his father Robert, whom he succeeded the next year. Ill-health would also probably account for the interruption of Richard Rowse's service as alderman.

Aldermen of the gild 1500-1542

1500	Robert Chapelyn
1501	William Chapelyn
1507	Richard Rowse
1511	Thomas Porter (Vicar)
1512	Edmund Kytmay
1513	Richard Rowse
1517	William Symonds
1520	Thomas Carrow
1524	William Flowerdew
1525	Adam Bishop (priest)
1533	John Symonds (priest)

The alderman of this gild certainly needed to be a person of some substance and social position, since the account book reveals that for several years the expenditure was larger than the annual income. The largest deficit for any year was in 1532 when priest Adam Bishop was called upon to find the sum of 32s 10d from his own resources. A specially appointed scribe was paid the sum of 8d per year for writing up these accounts, and for many years it was Thomas Dobbys.

One of the more pleasant duties of the alderman was to make the arrangements for the annual feast. Although specially elected feastmakers were responsible for providing the food at this event, the alderman needed to find a suitable venue for it. Normally such an occasion would be celebrated in the gildhall, but by 1509, the members of gild of the Nativity of the Blessed Virgin Mary had either found theirs too costly to maintain or no longer large enough. In 1448 it had sold a gildhall next to the market place to Thomas Payn, in return for which it was to receive an annual rent of 12s and be allowed to use the hall for three days between August 1st and September 29th. Since the gild's feast day was on September 8th, this was a very convenient arrangement, especially as the property could be repossessed if Thomas failed to keep it in a good state of repair. Another, possibly a larger, hall was purchased later and in 1495 almost £5 was spent on repairs to it, including a payment to Henry Seman for carrying timber "out of William Chapelyns yerde to the gylde hows". However, it was not difficult to find another venue for the feast. With the considerable overlap of gild membership, some people joining as many as five or more gilds, it was natural that there would be some co-operation between them, and the Gild of St. Thomas readily offered the use of their hall, in return for a payment of 16d, which was frequently spent on ale.

Reference has already been made to some of the team of lesser officials in this gild. In addition to the beadle, and the two feastmakers, a standard bearer and two collectors were also appointed, the latter to ensure that all payments for ingress fees, interest on stock, almsgiving and charges for the annual feast were forthcoming from the membership.

From the officials, we can now turn to the ordinary members. Who were they, and to what social groups did they belong? The first question is easily answered since we are fortunate enough to have a full list of entrants for the period 1497 to 1538, which has been included at the end of this chapter. A superficial examination of this list goes some way to answering the second question. It reveals that the members were divided between men and women roughly in the ratio three to two. Some of the men were priests and monks, while all the women were wives or widows of members. On some occasions wives joined at the same time as their husbands, while on others they followed a year or two later. Simple economics has often been given as the reason for this, but it is not the complete answer since members were allowed to spread the 12d individual entry fee over two or three years, and the Gild of the Nativity of the Blessed Virgin Mary employed the "special offer" arrangement, allowing husband and wife to enlist together at a joint fee of 20d. Payment by the instalment method was quite common, but not always regularly maintained, and there were times when the gild authorities felt action was necessary. In 1501, John Daundy and William Rowchester were appointed for the specific task of collecting all the outstanding debts. The list of members has also proved to be very important in filling particular gaps in our knowledge of the history of Wymondham. The abbot appointed in 1502, has, in all references to date, from Francis Blomefield in 1805 onwards, been named as Brother John, without a surname. It was of particular significance and very satisfying, therefore, to find the name Brother John Redmayne, Abbot of Wymondham, on the list of new entrants for 1510. Another interesting discovery was the references to William Irby. The membership list made in 1475 records the name of Sir William the schoolmaster as a new entrant for 1504. For the same year the 1509 version refers to Dom. William Ibry, which was probably mis-spelt, but indicates the provision of some education in the town at the very beginning of the sixteenth century. William could well have been the brother of Robert Irby vicar from 1479 to 1499. The Latin title "Dominus", reduced to Dom. in all membership lists was a courtesy title given to clerics who did not hold a degree. Another such courtesy title for clerics was "Sir" which should not be confused with its present-day usage.

We know from previous studies that relations between the regular clergy of the monastery and the secular clergy, the parish priests were not always cordial in Wymondham, but the early sixteenth century must have witnessed a period of comparative concord. The membership list contains the names of three successive vicars, Robert Irby, Thomas Porter and John Drye, as well as those of two abbots, John Redmayne and John Branforth. On joining the gild, all became governed by the rules established by the founders, one of which insisted that there should be no disharmony between members. The gild, therefore, served as a useful instrument in establishing good relations between the church and the convent in Wymondham. Such a high-powered membership must also mean that the gild held an important profile within the town.

Processions, with banner and candles, were an important feature of life in a gild, and it was natural that with constant use the gild banner would need replacing from time to time. Such a situation occurred in 1500, when the gild invited John Mayer to make a replacement. He was given precise details of the materials to be used, a mixture of stained cloth and pure silk, with a fringe of pure silk. The total cost of £3 10s was apparently found without much difficulty, indicating that there was no shortage of gild funds at this time. It may not seem much by today's standards, but we need to remember that in 1500 a labourer would be earning only 4d per day. It was considered a great honour to carry the gild banner in the processions within the town and for many years it was the responsibility of Richard Potter. He must have become somewhat of an expert in this field, since he acted as standard-bearer for three other gilds as well.

One feature of this gild was its commitment to the poorer members of the society, and it was the most generous of all the gilds for which we have evidence in this respect. Many testators leaving bequests referred to it as the gild of "our Lady of Pity". The offerings collected on the gild day were used to make these various payments to members who had fallen upon hard times, following the wishes of the gild's founders, which clearly stated that, for every 24d collected, 20d should be given to the poor of Wymondham and 4d to the lazars in Norwich. At times of particular distress, the gild of the Nativity of the Blessed Virgin Mary made extra contributions. In 1518, a difficult year in Wymondham, Agnes Woolterton received 20d, Thomas Plomer 20d, Alice Dyman 20d, John Colyour 21d, William Reve 24d and Thomas Reynold 21d. An additional sum of 24d was also allocated for general use among gild members, and the total cost of these

The Gild of the Nativity of the Blessed Virgin Mary

charitable bequests was 48d more than the entire collection for that year. Smaller, weekly sums were available on a more regular basis. The funds for these came from the 1½d paid by members at obit services and the annual ½d collected from all at the gild feast. Those who were sick, blind, lame or bed-ridden were given 7d per week if the funds amounted to 40s, and 3½d per week if it contained less. These payments to members were initiated by the founders to ensure that they "do not go out of the parish and do not become common beggars." When, in 1529, the "voluntary" donation for the poor was increased from ½d to 1d by the Election, there was no discussion on the matter. In a rather undemocratic manner, the members were told, clearly and firmly that "who so doth gainsay this shall forfeit one pound of wax."

Members were also encouraged to contribute regularly towards the cost of their own obit or funeral service. This pre-paid plan ensured that the burial, usually in the churchyard, but for anyone of sufficient importance within the walls of the abbey church, was carried out with due reverence and dignity. After a member died, all the brothers and sisters, with the gild banner and candles, were instructed by the beadle to process on the appointed day to the mass and subsequent burial. Only those who lived further than three miles from the parish of Wymondham were excused attendance at the service, where prayers were offered for the soul of the departed. In theory, expenses for these proceedings should have been met from the regular contributions made to the gild for this specific purpose, but here was another area where the members of this gild were not always prompt with their payments. In 1502 those behind with their obit money were issued with a warning that they should amend the situation "under the payne of a pound of wax paide at the next courte day" In 1500 the cost of an obit service had been 1s 6d; by 1507 it had risen to 2s.

had a gild hall next to the Market Place.

In addition to the charitable funds collected for specific purposes, income was also necessary for the day-to-day running of the gild. One of the most important sources of this revenue was the letting or "ferming" of lands and buildings. The gild of the Blessed Virgin Mary owned two tenantries near the market place, held of the manors of Cromwell and Choseley, and these were rented out for 7s 0d and 8s 0d per annum respectively.

We have seen that the close named "Odards", or "the Woderde close" was left to the gild by the will of Robert Chapelyn in 1500. It was rented initially to his son William for the special rate of 5s per annum if he maintained the gild lamp at his own cost. This sum was later increased to 12s, but this time without conditions. In 1512 the tenancy was taken over by William Symonds, a wealthy landowner, and it remained in the hands of the Symonds family unbroken until 1537. Priest John Symonds, William's elder son, took over temporarily on the death of his father and was then succeeded by his younger brother Henry for the next fifteen years. During all this time the annual rent remained at 12s. It is thought that the gild also owned a property in Damgate on or near the site of the present day Masonic Hall, according to an eighteenth century deed.

The Masonic Hall in Damgate – near the probable site of a property belonging to the Gild of the Nativity of the Blessed Virgin Mary

Other gild properties, described as large barns and stables, were also let and helped to provide a regular income in excess of 27s per annum. Further monies were generated by the sale of faggots, collected from the gild properties, and in 1526 seven members each purchased six score of them for 28d. A more profitable income was derived from the sale of wood from Odard's Close, and in 1538 20s was made for gild funds.

Analysis of Wymondham wills discloses that the Gild of the Blessed Virgin Mary was one of the most popular with the people of Wymondham when they considered the legacies they wished to make. In fact during the time between 1500 and the demise of the gilds, records reveal that it received a total of 32 bequests. Although the sums involved were not large, they nevertheless made a useful addition to general income. In a typical year (1518), William Reve left 6s 8d, Peter Bardwell 1s 8d, Thomas Reynold 12d, William Davy 1s 8d and Agnes Wolterton 3s 0d. Other income came in the form of wax from gild members who had disobeyed the regulations. The quantity of wax recorded in the account book from this source suggests that a number of the brothers and sisters failed to live up to the gild's high standards. A particularly heavy fine of 4lbs of wax was required if a member took his or her dispute with a fellow brother or sister to a court of law without allowing the alderman and the Election to try mediation first. Internal disagreements and subsequent litigation were particularly frowned upon by the gild. They created numerous problems within the gild itself, and did nothing to enhance its image in the wider community.

We have seen the importance of the letting of gild properties. Unfortunately, this largest source of income was also the greatest drain on its funds. The properties were in constant need of repair, and the account book contains many, many references to the fact. Broches and bindings, splints and straw, were all purchased in large quantities, and used for re-thatching roofs and re-building walls by the many skilled craftsmen and labourers of the town employed by the gild. Materials were re-cycled wherever possible, and when the roof of the "old house" was taken down in 1531 the sale of the timber brought in a total of 3s for the gild. Clay was carried by the cartload, and brick tiles bought to mend the floors of the tenantries. New wells were constructed and old ones repaired. All this activity is carefully recorded in minute detail in the account book, even down to the provision of a new well rope. Nor did the outgoings stop there. Hedging continuously needed maintenance and often replacing. In 1532, an entirely new hedge of 50 rods (approximately 275 yards) was constructed round one of the tenantries with thorns felled from other gild properties. The work was completed with the provision of a new gate with iron fastenings.

As to be expected, organisations in Wymondham were not exempt from national taxation, and a small but interesting feature in the account book links events in the town with those of the country as a whole. In 1513 the gild was requested to contribute 4d as a tax on its tenantries to the government, which was in the process of funding the young King Henry Vlll's ambitious expedition to France. Henry, very jealous of the French king, Francis l, was anxious to challenge his authority, and gain possessions in France, following the example of his forbears. The small sum required, however was not sufficient to have any impact on the gild accounts.

The highlight of the year for most members was the annual feast, details of which were communicated well in advance, by the alderman. The food was organised by the two feastmakers and paid for by the members themselves. Non-members were not allowed at this gathering, except the tenants of gild properties, who were invited at the gild's expense. What was actually eaten on this occasion we do not know, but no doubt it would have been similar to that consumed by the Gild of the Holy Trinity, details of which we shall see later. After the meal, it was customary for some light entertainment to be arranged, usually in the form of minstrels and jugglers. Occasionally there were additional items, and in 1510 there must have been considerable excitement when a live ape was included. The pleasures of the feast were short lived, however, and it was back to reality the following day, to attend the dirge and requiem mass for the souls of the departed brothers and sisters. Throughout the service, as indeed at all times, the candle in front of the image of the Virgin would be burning.

The activities of the gild of the Blessed Virgin Mary were much reduced in the years following the dissolution of the smaller monasteries. The last entrant, the wife of William Stokton, is recorded as having joined in 1538. The last alderman, John Symonds, a priest, was appointed in 1534, and continued to be responsible for the limited events of the gild until the early 1540s. There is evidence that it was still functioning in 1544, although the last recorded bequest was made by the vicar, John Drye, in 1537. In 1540 the two gild tenantries were sold to Robert Seman and John Neve for £15, but the gild still possessed and rented out Odards Close as late as 1544. The members of the gild had stipulated that the proceeds from the 1540 sale should go to the parish church of Wymondham for "the payments of our sovren lord kyng for the stepell of our Lady Chapel the building over hokmas ile with certen grownd and ledde bowht by the inhabitants of the seid town of Wymondham of our seid sovren Lord Kyng sometime belongyng to the seid Abbey of Wymondham."

A view of Hockmas Aisle (South Aisle)

This was one of several transactions between the parish and the king to buy parts of the former Abbey for the use of the town. It was also one of the last official duties of the Gild of the Blessed Virgin Mary in the town. No doubt the members were sad to see its demise. Robert Stokton and his wife Alice, two of the last to join, had obviously enjoyed gild membership and seeing the forthcoming closure of the gild of the Nativity of the Blessed Virgin Mary, transferred their allegiance to the Gild of Saint John the Baptist in 1540 and 1541 respectively. Thomas Carrow followed their example in 1544.

List of members of the Gild of the Nativity of the Blessed Virgin Mary

Compiled 1509 Richard Rowse, Alderman

M. Robert Irby vicar
Stephen Glydby
Dom. Thomas Bacon
Nicholas Mekyllfeld
Richard Ironhed and wife
Clement Wyllyngton
Thomas Plomer
James Colyour
Agnes Fox
William Davy and wife
Thomas Dobbys
Henry Seman
Dom. Richard Rowse
John Lovyk
John Dixon
Thomas Cheseman
John Kensey and wife
Thomas Weende and wife
Peter Belys and wife
Thomas Knyght
William Dowsyng
Stephen Seman

1498
William Symonde

1499
Dom. Thomas Dalys
John Harold
Wife of John Dawndy
William Caly

1500
William Rowchester and wife
Joanna wife of John Dixon
John Mayour

1501
Dom. Robert Nelyng
Edmund Appleyard
James Frosdyk
Joanna his wife
John Olyve
Agnes his wife
Margaret Harold
Edmund Kytmay
Amelia his wife
Joanna Symonde
wife of John Flye

1502
John Bale
Richard Dyman
Henry Martyn
Robert Toly
Richard Alden

1503
Francis Sothewell
Alice Lovyk

1504
John Gryffyn
Isabel wife of Robert Toly
Dom. William Irby
Oliver Heed

1505
Thomas Lombe
John Randolf
Isabel Bale
Isabel wife of Henry Martyn
Thomas Carrowe
Thomas Luce

1507
Rosa wife of Thomas Lombe
Agnes Cheseman
Margaret Spyllysby

1508
William Walter

1509
Robert Kensy
Joanna Chapelyn widow
Richard Male and his wife
William Flowerdew
Katherine his wife
William Wurlyngton and his wife
John Colyour and his wife
John Gorham and his wife
Robert Gylforde
Stephen Borrell

1510
John Redmayne Abbot of
        Wymondham
Thomas Porter vicar
Peter Bardwell chaplain
Robert Sterlyng
Alice wife of Richard Dyman
Isabella Pulham
Alice wife of Robert Sterlyng
Johanna Wurlyngton
Agnes Wulterton

1511
William Reve
Henry Appilton
Robert Seman
Margaret Mannyng

1512
Richard Botye
Thomas Mortymer

1513
Robert Woodward
Wife of James Collyor
Wife of Thomas Mortymer

1514
M. John Drye vicar
Thomas Reynold
Alice Reynold
Robert Wyseman sen
Phillippa Dynnis
Wife of Robert Kensy
Dom. John Symondes

1515
Robert Baxter
Isabel his wife
William Teteshal
Alice his wife
Alice wife of Thomas Luce
Dom. Adam Bishopp

1516
Robert Dynne
Wife of Robert Wiseman
Wife of Thomas Knyght

1517
John Branfort Abbot of
        Wymondham
William Bettes
Thomas Fawce
Thomas Candelere

1518
John Dynn
John Kensey jun
John Flowerdew
Thomas Dynnys
Edmund Hamont
Margaret Angell
wife of Richard Alden

1519
wife of John Kensey sen
wife of John Kensey jun
Dom. Robert Frosdyk
William Shere
William Smythe
Richard Colyour

1520
Thomas Cheteryng
William Carter of Carleton Rode
William Reynolds jun
Wife of Thomas Cheteryng
Thomas Luce jun

1521
Stephen Vardon
Richard Toly
Agnes his wife
Richard Potter

1522
Henry Symonds
Robert Bale
John Mekyllfeld
Katherine his wife

1523
Agnes Flouerdew
Clara Cheteryng

1524
Josiah Kyllyngworth
Margaret his wife
Robert Seman
wife of John Carter of Carleton
        Rode
Nicholas Stokton
Margery his wife
Robert Vekere
Katherine Vyntner
Matilda Bell
Wife of Robert Seman
Margaret Vekere
John Mannyng taylor
William Burges
Thomas Yongman

1525
Thomas Sterlyng
Margaret his wife
Thomas Wiseman
Margaret Symondes

1526
wife of Robert Dyn
wife of Thomas Wiseman

1528
Thomas Waschyngton
William Lombe gent
Elizabeth Chantrell widow
Wife of John Flowerdew
Katherine Reynolds
Dom. John Gonned
William Newson
Geoffrey Gombe

1529
Dom. Roger Randolf
William Mekyllfeld
Richard English
William Wiseman
Katherine Fedymont widow
Robert Ensyng gent
Agnes his wife
Katherine Mekyllfeld
Elizabeth Newsom

1530
Henry Dyman
Elizabeth English
Wife of William Wiseman

1531
John Fischpond
Wife of William Lombe gent
Katherine Dyman

1534
Dom. John Pyncheon
Dom. William Bukk

1535
Richard Bron

1536
Robert Stokton

1537
Robert Kempley
Johanna Wiseman

1538
wife of Robert Stokton

Over leaf – A page from the accounts of the Gild of St John the Baptist (1524) in a mixture of Latin and English.

Compotus. Johannis Symondes [illegible] Aldernam [?] [illegible] in Anno Domini millesimo quingentesimo vicesimo quarto et regni Regis Henrici octavi xvj[mo]

De rec[eptis]

Item primo rec — iij s x d — de potellis sold [?] by John [illegible] [illegible] et [illegible]
Item rec — ij s vij d — de potts sold by [illegible] et William [illegible] / fforden
Item rec — xiiij d — ex [illegible] ultimo compoto

Summa — vij s vij d

De ingressu [?]

Item primo rec — iiij d — de Stephen [illegible] pro ingr[essu] — iij s iiij d
Item rec — vj d — de Roberto Bristowe pro ingr[essu] — v s — Thoma [illegible] pleg[ius]

Summa — x d

De ffirma

Item primo rec — xiij s iiij d — de Willelmo [illegible] pro firma [illegible]
Item rec — ij s — in plenam firmam [illegible] pro ultimo anno de Thoma [illegible]
Item rec — iij s — de [illegible] Thoma in parte solucionis — vij s pro firma [illegible]
Item rec — iij s vj d — de Willelmo [illegible] in parte solucionis — vij s vj d pro firma [illegible]
Item rec — ij s — de [illegible] pro firma [illegible]
Item rec — x d — de Galfrido Symondes pro firma [illegible]

Summa — xxvj s viij d

Summa totalis omnium receptorum — xxxvj s j d
inde [illegible]

De solucionibus

Item primo sol — xij d — for a new [illegible] to the [illegible] to the [illegible]
Item sol — xij d — for iij loads of clay to a [illegible]
Item sol — ij s vj d — to John [illegible] making the [illegible]
Item sol — xxxiij s iiij d — to [illegible] in parte of payment for [illegible]
Item sol — x d — to the [illegible] of [illegible] for the [illegible]

Summa — xxxviij s viij d

THE GILD OF ST. JOHN THE BAPTIST

The idea of dedicating a gild to St. John the Baptist might seem rather surprising. Very little is known about his life, apart from the stories of his birth and death and the occasion on which he baptised Jesus in the River Jordan. These few incidents were, nevertheless, very colourful and dramatic, and extremely popular in the mystery plays of the period, especially the roles of Herod and Salome. This, together with his timely birthday of Midsummer Day, may partially explain the number of gilds choosing him as a patron. The parishes of Wymondham, and Swaffham both had a gild dedicated to St. John the Baptist at this time, and in many ways the two seem to have been organised on similar lines. The main source of our evidence in Wymondham is the account book which covers the period from 1500 until 1547, when Richard Pynnar, its last member, joined. At the front of this is a list of those who were established members in 1504, together with those who joined between 1506 and 1547, apart from an unexplained gap between 1519 and 1530. This record includes many women who often joined at the same time as their husbands, rather than later, the usual practice in other Wymondham gilds. The reason for this may well be related to the little emphasis placed on ingress money in the accounts, which meant that entry depended on the wishes of a couple rather than their financial resources.

The 1504 list of members, reproduced at the end of this chapter, includes twelve married couples, the Vicar, Robert Irby, three women who were probably widows, and eight men. The wives of two of these eight, Margaret Mannyng and Catherine Hogan, joined later. Other later entrants were successive vicars, Thomas Porter, John Drye and Doctor Henry King. Of the regular clergy, Abbot John Kyrtelyng was an active member, and became alderman in 1500. The usual process of a son following his father into a gild does not appear to have always been the case here, and occasionally a son pre-empted his father's decision to join. William Caly junior, together with his wife, Alice, joined the gild in 1504, while William, senior, and his wife Isabella followed in 1507.

The basic offices, rules and observances of the Gild of St. John the Baptist were similar to those of the gild of the Nativity of the

Blessed Virgin Mary. In addition to the alderman and the usual council of twelve, however, two other members were chosen annually. These were probably reserves or trainees, since they almost always went on to become official members of the twelve later. The other officers, including standard bearer, custodian of the light, beadle, stewards and collectors for the alms monies, were all appointed at the same time on the gild day. A member usually served for a period in one of the lesser positions before being elected to the council of twelve, where he remained for many years. John Joby junior was a good example of this. Chosen originally as a feastmaker, he went on to serve for twenty-seven years on the council between 1505 and 1537. For some of these years his father, another John, was a member of the "twelve". Yet another John, John Symonds, provides us with a further example of long service: he was alderman for twenty years and chaplain for even more.

Members were very conscientious regarding their attendance at the parades and gild masses and requiems for all the departed gild members. Rather surprisingly, they were less diligent about attending the annual feast, and in 1513 gild officials were forced to remind them of their obligation to do so. Further encouragement to obey this rule was provided by the introduction of a 10s fine for those failing to present themselves on this occasion. The effectiveness of such a threat can be measured by the lack of entries in the account book recording the receipt of any such sums.

One of the more important practices of any gild, that of providing a constant light before the image of the patron saint, was carefully followed, and a candle continuously burned before the image of St. John until 1540. Up to this time the annual cost for this service varied between 8d and 3s. The increase was not constant or regular; it rose gradually to 3s in 1523 and then decreased to 2s 4d in six years, followed by a small increase to 2s 8d in 1537. The lack of reference to lights after 1540 indicates that the gild was conforming to the most recent of Henry VIII's legislation which forbade, not the provision of images, but the provision of lights before them.

The main body of the parish church was the centre of the gild's religious activites until 1509, when it was decided to make a separate altar or chapel for St. John. The gild agreed to help in the construction of this, and paid Thomas Sterling and William Bale 40s as a part payment for "the stuff and makyng of the seid chapel". Such a move was in keeping with similar constructions made by the more wealthy gilds in the country at this time. The altar in the chapel was made of wood, stone and iron. Later, Edmund Kytmay provided a buckram curtain, and a corporas case was made. It would be very exciting to think that it was the one still held in the muniment room of Wymondham Abbey, but unfortunately it is not, as that one dates back to the thirteenth century.

The Wymondham Corporas Case (used to hold the cloth on which the vessels containing the consecrated elements were placed during the celebration of Mass) It is made of coarse canvas or linen with embroidered armorial designs in blue, yellow and white

Work continued on the gild chapel the following year, when curtains and altar cloths were provided and hallowed, and an altar table was commissioned. The image of the "hed of Saint John" was also repainted.

Most gilds possessed their own furniture and utensils, which they used for the annual feast and drinkings. Some of those owned by St. John are recorded in the accounts for the year 1504, from which we learn that the gild owned five tables, approximately five yards long, of which one was made of oak and two others were described as being for "the common people"; a hint of hierarchy here? Four forms of the same length were used in conjunction with the tables, and further seating was available in the form of stools, which apparently needed constant repair.

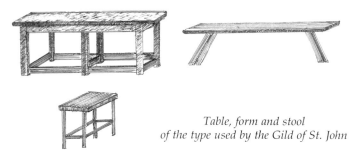

*Table, form and stool
of the type used by the Gild of St. John*

Gild utensils included two iron spits, a large brass pot, two latten basins and a pewter salt cellar. Salt played a very important part in the diets of people at this time, both as a preservative and for additional flavouring. The range of utensils recorded is rather limited when compared with the 1496 list made at Swaffham. This had included saucers, dishes and trenchers, some of which were marked with the initial letter of the gild, and seventeen wooden spoons. There is also a reference to the four long tablecloths it proudly possessed. The omission of such items in the Wymondham gild inventory does not necessarily mean that it did not possess them, it could have simply been that the inventory was compiled for a different purpose, perhaps to list those utensils used for food preparation. Indeed, it would have been very surprising for there not to have been any wooden spoons available in Wymondham, since they were manufactured within the parish itself, at Spooner Row.

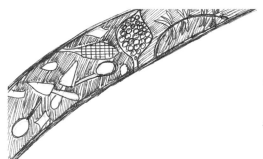

Carving from the Wymondham Market Cross rebuilt after the fire of 1615 illustrating the spoons and spigots made locally

All these items would have been in great demand for the annual feast, which always occurred in spite of the reluctance of some members to attend. The number of tables and gild lists suggest that in some years there could well have been well over fifty members present. We have no record from this gild of what was actually on the menu, but no doubt it would have included items such as "beef, mutton, lamb, pork and goose with sauce, spices, bread cheese and ale", which were recorded by the Swaffham gild. The meal was followed in the customary manner with entertainment by a

40

minstrel, who could well have been Thomas Bylawe, a famous "wayte of the towne", who often offered his services to the gilds.

Stock holding was a particular feature of the gild at the very beginning of the sixteenth century. From a list, made in 1500, of all the borrowing members, we can see that the gild had sufficient assets to issue stock to the value of £11 18s 9d. This sum was divided between thirty members. Among the more well-known of these were the Abbot, John Kyrtelyng, and Thomas Hogan, who had been a churchwarden in 1494. Unfortunately, both died before their stock could be repaid, and it was left to other gild members to settle their outstanding debts, over a period of two or three years. Women were given stock rarely, but it is not clear whether this was by intention or because of the lack of interest on their part. The only woman on the 1500 list of stockholders was Agnes Blexter, who, together with her husband, had stock to the value of 6s 8d, and for whom the Vicar stood guarantor. Loans of stock seem to have peaked in 1500, when the interest accrued amounted to 20s. After this, the gild became more interested in using its resources for buying and renting property than offering them for straightforward loans. Thus the stock holdings, together with the income on them, gradually decreased as the gild turned its attention to the more lucrative investment in the renting or "ferming" of its buildings and lands. Changing attitudes toward the holding of land were taking place in the country as a whole at this time, and the long-established idea that land was held in trust within a family, to be passed down to future generations, became less important than profit-making, in the changing national economic climate. Consequently, a land market became established, and the Gild of St John the Baptist was quick to take advantage of it, extending its ownership of land and cottages for renting. The extent and comparative success of this policy can be seen from the detailed tables (below), showing the main items of income and expenditure of the gild. The acquisition of properties was a continuous process. In 1502 the Gild of St. John the Baptist was already renting Arnold Close, held of the manor of Grishaugh, and let for 10s per annum. This rent gradually increased to 15s in 1542, when the tenants, Elizabeth Hobbys and John Carre, were given the additional responsibility for the hedging and ditching of the property. At the beginning of the century, two other parcels of land were regularly rented out at 8d and 10d per annum.

Date	Rent from lands	Interest from stock	Stock repayment	Drinkings
1501	10s	31s 5d		
1502	12s 6d	26s 8d	6s 8d	
1503	30s 10d	15s 11d	33s 4d	
1504	24s	19s 8d		
1505		17s 11d	24s 4d	
1506	11s	19s 3d		
1507	3s 4d	20s	6s 8d	
1508	13s 2d	11s		
1509	13s 2d	12s 2d	26s 8d	15s 8d
1510	12s 10d	10s 10d	5s	25s 4d
1511	12s 10d	10s 6d	18s 4d	
1512	12s 10d	7s 7d	27s	
1513	12s 10d	7s 5d	18s 4d	
1514	12s 10d	7s	10s 9d	10s
1515	12s 10d	6s	15s 11d	10s 11d
1516	19s 6d	4s 8d	11s 8d	
1517	19s 6d	4s 6d	3s 3d	7s
1518	19s 6d	3s 7d	6s 8d	16s 2d
1519	19s 6d	2s 10d	3s 4d	
1520	21s 2d	1s 8d	15s	
1521	23s	1s 6d		9s 2d
1522	24s 10d	10d		2s6d
1523	19s 2d	10d		12s
1524	28s 8d	10d		6s 4d
1525	30s 10d	10d		
1526	32s 10d	10d		12s 6d
1527	21s	10d		5s 2d
1528	30s 8d	10d		
1529	23s 2d	10d	13s 4d	5s 8d
1530	30s 8d	10d	13s 4d	
1531	24s 2d	10d		5s 3d
1532	37s 2d	10d		2s 4d
1533	33s 2d	10d		
1534	22s 2s	10d		5s 2d
1535	38s 2d	10d		5s 6d
1536	22s 2d	10d		5s 10d
1537	34s 2d	10d		5s
1538	30s 2d	10d		8s 8d
1539	13s 4d sold land	6d		
1540	13s 4d	10d		
1541	13s 4d			4s 3d
1542	13s 4d			
1543	5s			

In 1512, the gild accelerated this policy of acquiring further properties, and purchased a house in Downham Street from John Joby senior, which had previously belonged to Richard Payn and was held of the manor of the Abbey. Of the total cost, 20s was paid to John Joby that year, and the remaining 43s 4d, in instalments, by 1516. Additional land was purchased in 1515 from John Reynberd. In 1521 the annual income from rents rose to 23s, now including another house sometimes referred to as a "granary". Three years later a further cottage, in Rustens manor, was bought by the gild from Joan Joby, the wife of William Joby, for 70s. The payment, once again, was spread over a period of time, in this case three years. This cottage was also eventually rented out. But it was not all pure profit. The table of expenditure also reveals the large sums of money which had to be spent to keep the newly-acquired properties in a reasonable state of repair. In some years, this meant that the alderman had to carry a considerable financial burden, as the gild accounts went into deficit. Alterations as well as repairs were undertaken, and the house bought from John Joby was fitted with a partition and re-thatched. One part was then used as a gildhall, the probable venue for the annual feast, and the other part was rented out. Unfortunately, we are unable to locate it precisely, but appears to have been within the town. Further outlays were also necessary to repair the second new cottage, which needed re-thatching, a new cope for the chimney, and a new corbel and ropes for the well.

Older properties also continued to need repair. In 1527 the gild was forced to spend over 50s on the construction of a new chimney and the re-thatching of a cottage. Maintenance of grounds, such as the cutting of thorns and the mending of hedges and gates was an additional and constant drain on resources. The payments for rents to other gilds and repairs in 1533 amounted to 63s, leaving a shortfall of 30s for the alderman John Symonds to bear. Much of the expense in this year was the result of work on the wall at the end of "the old halle" and a new roof to the "bakhouse"(backhouse). A small sum was given to Mr. Banyard for an entry and copy for another newly acquired parcel of pastureland, of the manor of Grishaugh. It took another year before this debt was cleared and it was not long before further outlays were necessary. The great door in the hall was "walled up" and more thatching was required.

Special fen thatch from Bawburgh costing 2s 10d per load, was brought into the town, while further and cheaper supplies from Melton were purchased at only 2s 4d per load. Responsibility for all the thatching was left to Thomas Hempshale and his servant between 1527 and 1536, who worked for at least sixteen days during the final year.

As a direct result of the dissolution of the monasteries, the gild came to a very important decision, to help the town with its purchase of crucial parts of the old abbey. On April 28th 1539 the brethren agreed to sell their house with attached yards in Downham to Thomas Donton for 20 marks. This sum was duly presented to the "church of Wymondham" for payment to the king for the steeple (tower) over the lady chapel, quantities of lead, and some grounds which had previously belonged to the Abbey, but had passed to the crown on its dissolution. Arnold Close and all the other gild properties were retained but little was spent on them after this.

Where had the funds come from to embark upon this concerted move to purchase property? We have seen that payment over time had been necessary to buy some of them, but much of the finance had come from the retention of stock as it was paid off by members. In addition to this stock, the gild had a number of small but regular sources of income from entrance fees, drinkings, and legacies. In addition, the gild did not appear to worry unduly about balancing its annual accounts, and for nineteen years between 1511 and 1538, the alderman carried a deficit of between 7d and 58s 2d, the latter being a very large sum for any individual to bear. Drinkings in fact proved to be a lucrative source of income and a pleasant one too. The first of these took place in 1509, the year of the accession of King Henry VIII. They were usually organised by comparatively new entrants to the gild, probably as an alternative to entrance fees. Leading figures in the town, such as Vicars John Drye and Dr. Henry King did not escape this tradition, and were responsible for drinkings, with other members in 1517 and 1541 respectively. Rather surprisingly, the 1517 drinking was not held in the recently purchased gild house, but in a hall rented from the gild of St. Thomas.

EXPENDITURE - GILD OF ST. JOHN THE BAPTIST

Date	General Expenses	Cost of Repairs	Stock given for interest	Purchase of land	Sum in debt to alderman
1501	9s 7d				
1502	9s 8d				
1503	8s 11d	15s 11d	16s 8d		
1504	12s 10d	10s 8d	19s		
1505	14s 1d		10s 4d		
1506	12s 6d	29s 2d	8s		
1507	23s	6d	3s 4d		
1508	18s 6d				
1509	17s 11d	72s 10d			
1510	16s 4d	38s 4d			
1511	17s 6d	15s 8d			
1512	16s 10d	65s 9d			8s 8d
1513	14s 7d	15s 7d		20s	
1514	18s	14s 4d		10s	
1515	14s 9d	18s 5d		10s	
1516	18s 2d	21s 10d		23s 4d	22s 10d
1517	15s	14s 2d			17s 10d
1518	16s 1d	5s 8d		30s	22s 4d
1519	16s 10d	13s 4d			31s 2d
1520	16s	2s 11d			11s 9d
1521	16s				
1522	16s	11s 7d		31s 8d	
1523	16s 4d	14s 8d			
1524	18s	4s 6d		34s 2d	7d
1525	16s 5d	13s 3d		21s 11d	36s 5d
1526	17s 1d	7s 11d		16s 8d	33s 2d
1527	16s 1d	56s 1d			58s 2d
1528	12s 3d	18s 1d			57s 7d
1529	14s				38s 2d
1530	14s 9d	16s 7d			18s 4d
1531	13s 9d	10d			2s 9d
1532	13s 9d	5s 10d			
1533	15s 9d	56s		7s 8d	29s 7d
1534	14s	11s 4d			26s 10d
1535	14s 6d				
1536	15s 2d	35s 5d			8s 8d
1537	14s 2d	40s 4d			23s 3d
1538	14s 4d	9d			3s 2d
1539	14s 3d				
1540	10s 3d				
1541	9s 8d				
1542	10s 3d				
1543	10s 7d				

Legacies from past members made a useful but not a great contribution to gild funds, with sums ranging from 6d to 6s 8d. Altogether twenty-four bequests are recorded in the wills available to us, which puts the gild of St. John the Baptist in the group of the four most popular for attracting bequests. The close connection between the gild and certain families is evident. Legacies from father and son, both called William Caly, were recorded in 1509 and 1530, and five members of the Metyngham family left bequests between 1501 and 1538. Since it was common practice for people to belong to more than one gild, not all could benefit when a member died. For example, the vicar, John Drye, who joined this gild in 1515, made a drinking for it two years later, and served on the Election for many years, made bequests to the gilds of St. Thomas, St. Peter, Our Ladies Light and the Nativity of the Blessed Virgin Mary, but left nothing to the Gild of St. John the Baptist.

A separate fund was established for alms and funeral costs, the operation of which was the responsibility of two members appointed for this specific purpose. No details of the income received, apart from yearly totals, are recorded, but sums of between 16d and 20d were paid out for individual members at their decease. Every year a further sum was paid for prayers to be said for the souls of "all the brethren and sisters of thys gyld departed owt of this transitory liff".

Several interesting and long-serving members of the gild of St. John the Baptist merit special mention. Thomas Cheeseman, alderman for eighteen years between 1503 and 1523, was one of the largest stockholders in 1500, and rented the gild property, Arnold Close, in partnership with other members, for nine years. Other gild properties were also in his employ from time to time. John Joby junior followed his father, of the same name, into office within the gild. Alderman in 1508 and 1509, he served as one of the twelve electors every year between 1513 and 1537. He also supplied and carried straw for the thatching of gild properties. Stephen Platemaker, a 4d a day labourer, was often employed on hedging and ditching by the gild. On several occasions, he also supplied straw, broches and bindings for thatching. Given a small amount of gild stock in 1504, he paid his 4d interest regularly every year until 1539. His position as a member of the Election for twenty-eight years illustrates the diversity of social status within the gild.

The Hobbys family were comparatively wealthy, and featured prominently in the gild records. Thomas and his wife Elizabeth must have joined during the period 1520 to 1530, for which we have no details of new entrants. At the time of his death in 1535, Thomas owned forty-three acres of land, his dwelling house which was enfeoffed jointly to him and his wife Elizabeth, a cottage lying beyond Downham Hall and another "place and lands", which he purchased just before his death. He had also rented Arnold Close for nine years up to this time and his widow continued the tenancy for a further nine years to the end of the account book. Thomas Hobbys was also able to leave considerable sums of money to his four daughters and two sons. After his death, Elizabeth had the distinction of becoming the only woman in all the gild accounts to be named as a gild office-holder, when she became one of the feastmakers in 1539. Her two sons, Robert and John were among the last recorded members to join the gild in 1541 and 1544. Elizabeth Hobbys continued to manage her lands successfully and we next read of her in the Churchwardens' Accounts where, in 1553, she is recorded as giving 20s for the repairs to the north and south aisles and the porch of the parish church. Her son Robert became a churchwarden in 1552, and also contributed to the same repairs. Seven years later, the gift of another 20s to the churchwardens from "Mother Hobbys" is probably from the same Elizabeth.

The activities of the gild of St. John the Baptist declined rapidly after the sale of the gild properties in 1539 and the donation of the proceeds to the parish. It continued to attract new members, but there was a marked reluctance to hold office within in it. This meant that new entrants were forced to accept office in the same year in which they joined, and long-standing members had to be persuaded back into positions of responsibility. In the dying years of the gild, the membership concentrated on raising money for almsgiving, arranging the annual drinkings, and holding funeral obits. It continued to attract new members until 1547, often from other gilds which had ceased to function, but the last accounts were written in 1544.

Names of brothers and sisters of the Gild of St. John the Baptist, written in 1504

Master Robert Irby vicar
Thomas Cheeseman
Agnes his wife
Richard Payn
Letitia his wife
Agnes Wolterton
Richard Platemaker
Margaret his wife
Thomas Cook
Catherine his wife
Isabella Fox
John Ston
Isabella his wife
Thomas Fauce
Margaret his wife
William Burgess
Matilda his wife
Nicolas Hogon
William Brondale
John Joby sen
Joanna his wife
John Lytyll
Agnes his wife
Stephen Platemaker
Richard Gilden
Robert Bristow
Marion his wife
Agnes Hood
Thomas Coliour
William Caly jun
Alice his wife
John Petit
Christina his wife
John Mannyng John Reynolds
John Kensy jun

Entrants 1506

Richard Reynolds
John Lawys
Margaret his wife
John Joby jun
Katherine his wife
Thomas Churche
Isabella his wife
John Medillton
Margaret his wife
John Clerke
Richard Fox
Peter Belys
Alice his wife
Margaret Mannyng
John Rudd

Entrants 1507

William Caly sen
Isabella his wife
Margaret Blexter

Entrants 1508

John Symonds chaplain
Geoffrey Symond
Thomas Hendry
John Fedymont
Joanna his wife
Stephen Platemaker

Entrants 1510

Thomas Porter vicar
John Jordon
Robert Wiseman jun
Thomas Caly

Entrants 1511

Catherine wife of Nicolas Hogan
Rowland Newton
Isabella his wife
Agnes wife of John Mydylton
Thomas Mortymer
Christina wife of Robert Wiseman
        jun
Thomas Bron
Robert Gylforth

Entrants 1512

Robert Woodward
Isabella his wife
Richard Dayns
Alice his wife
Margery wife of John Reynberd
John Bale
Margaret wife of Thomas Caly

Entrants 1513

Margaret wife of Geoffrey
        Symonds
Isabella Hendry
Catherine wife of John Lytyll

Entrants 1514

William Caly

Entrants 1515

John Drye vicar
Robert Gylden

Entrants 1516

John Hendry al Sponer
William Hodson
Agnes his wife

Entrants 1517

Roger Symond
Elizabeth his wife
Richard Caly

Entrants 1518

Anna wife of Geoffrey Symonds

Entrants 1519

John Caly
Joanna his wife
Batholomew Hamont
Isabella wife of John Fedymont
Isabella wife of John Bale

(Entrants 1520 – 1529 no entries)

Entrants 1530

Dom. John Connell
John Alen
Agnes his wife
Robert Gronde
John Marrowe
Thomas Marsham
Agnes his wife
John Baxter
Richard Caly
William Wynter
Alice his wife
Robert Iole
Margaret his wife

Entrants 1531

Johanna Deynes

Entrants 1532

John Symond
John Legett
Joanna his wife
John Bryce
Beatrix his wife
John a Banke
Margaret wife of Richard Caly
Wife of William Caly

Entrants 1533

John Payn
Margaret wife of John Symond

Entrants 1534

William Stockton
William Joby
Joanna his wife

Entrants 1535

Robert Dyn
Robert Fauce
John Wacy

Entrants 1536

Dom.Thomas Okdeyn
John Metyngham
Thomas Wenlock

Entrants 1537

Dom. Richard Desdam
Stephen Horby
Catherine his wife
John Cuschen
Robert Smyth alias Folsham
John Fynk jun.
Joanna his wife
Elizabeth Newton widow

Entrants 1540

Mr. Henry Kyng Doctor of
         Divinity
M. William Ballard chaplain
Nicholas Kett
Thomas Kett senior
Wife of John Alen
Robert Stockton

Entrants 1541

William Castleton
Joanna his wife
William Frosdyk
Agnes his wife
Richard Howse
John Carre
Alice his wife
Alice wife of Robert Stockton
William Clerk
William Stevynson
John Hobbys
Agnes his wife
Thomas Woode
Agnes Cuschen

Entrants 1542

John Harvy
Alice his wife
Barthomew Howse
Sibilla his wife
John Hogges
Margaret Howse
Catherine Stevynson
Elizabeth Quentryell
John Fedymont

Entrants 1543

Robert Carne
Joanna his wife
Thomas Uttyng
Henry Fosse
Stephen Vikyn
Catherine his wife
Richard Lightwyn

Entrants 1544

Thomas Carrow
John Skere
John Cok
Geoffrey Sturman
Elizabeth his wife
Henry Alexander
Robert Wetyn
Thomas Whitlawe
Richard Smythe
Lucy Sturman
Robert Hobbys
Robert Carre
Joanna his wife

Entrants 1547

Richard Pynnar

THE GILD OF ALL SAINTS

The Gild of All Saints enjoyed many features common to the others in Wymondham at this time, but it also developed some interesting characteristics of its own. Again much of our evidence is based on the gild account book, which covers the years from 1501 to 1536, and contains the membership lists for the first year. It also reveals that the rules, the office holders and the activities were in line with those gilds we have already discussed.

Once more, the list of members proves to be very helpful, the first page of which is reproduced at the beginning of this book. It is headed by Robert Irby, still referred to as the vicar, although he had been replaced by Thomas Porter by this time. His name is followed by 29 married couples, and three females, possibly widows, Margery Denton, Margaret Hynde and Agnes Newland. Ten individual males complete the list. Two were clergy, and the wives of two others, Rose Foster and Margaret Dobbys, joined later, although by this time Rose was a widow. Thus we can see that the actual membership in 1502 was the original 71 plus 5 new entrants, making a total of 76, although we cannot be certain that all were active at any one time. The subsequent entries of second wives reveal an enthusiasm on the part of widowers to enrol their new spouses into full membership. It has been suggested that some members joined with the intention of seeking a new husband or wife, but there is little evidence to suggest that this was the case in Wymondham. Richard Kiddell's first wife Margaret joined the Gild of All Saints in 1525 but died two years later. Her successor, Christina, became a member in 1530 and hosted a drinking the following year. Sometimes a husband was so keen to enrol his wife in the gild that he, like William Blythe, donated a bushel of malt to celebrate the occasion.

Apart from the vicar, the only other member of the clergy on the original 1501 list is Thomas Dalys, who is described as a chaplain. Further evidence, however, reveals that later on there was much more involvement in this gild by the clergy, both regular and secular, than in the others we have considered over the same period. It is not always entirely clear to which section of the clergy they belonged, but it appears that no fewer than 15 not only joined the gild, but also played an active part in its life. In 1529 and 1530 three of the Election were clergy while the pivotal role of Alderman was conferred on James Curson, a monk, for two years, and upon priests Thomas Dalys, Robert Frosdyk and John Drye for two, five, and seven years respectively. This adds further support to our evidence of harmonious relations between the two groups of clergy at this time, since both were committed to the gild rules of co-operation and brotherly love.

The Gild of All Saints engaged in the usual activities expected of such an organisation. In addition to the post of alderman, the officers appointed included the beadle, two collectors of alms money, two feastmakers, a standard bearer and the custodian of the light. The gild feast was celebrated regularly, followed by the dirge on the following Monday. Gild members were all expected to contribute ½d each on this occasion. Donations were made annually to the lepers at the gates of Norwich, and less regularly to the poor in the surrounding area. Items recorded in the account book reveal that, in 1519, 1d was given to a "pore syke man", and a "pore pryst" was helped in 1522. The gild light was constantly maintained before what in one source was described as "all saintes", and in another as "the crucifix". Other outgoings from the funds included sums for mending candlesticks and torches, and rewarding the sextons for ringing the bell for gild functions.

Life in this gild was not always without its problems. In 1509 the alderman Thomas Dalys died whilst in office and the gild was thrown into disarray. No accounts were written for the following year, and the members obviously decided that it was necessary to take some measure to deal with a similar situation occurring in the future. James Frosdyk, a fellow priest, was appointed to fill the vacant post of alderman on the condition that "yff he dey the seid gild shall have 6s 8d". It is not clear why this precaution was necessary, but it may have been to cover any gild funds the alderman had in his possession when he died. This was not the case with Thomas Dalys, however, since the gild funds were in surplus at the time of his death.

Another problem was the apparent reluctance of gild members to hold office, or, perhaps, to hold certain offices. Many preferred to pay a fine rather than take on gild responsibilities. In 1501 John Baxter had donated a chetyll (kettle) so that he might be "discharged of holding of the seid gylde". Robert Ringer paid 4s in instalments during 1526 to be excused from the post of feastmaker "for all time", while John Sygar, on entering the gild, managed to be excused from all office-holding for a mere 3s 4d. By 1528 the cost of escaping these onerous burdens had risen to 5s, as John Cotyngham found to his cost. Thomas Sendell was unlucky. He did not manage to avoid his appointment as alderman in 1530, but was able to make a discreet withdrawal from office the same year. For some reason the gild generously allowed him to do so "free and peacefully". Another Thomas, Thomas Carrow, found the position of feastmaker too burdensome, and Henry Dyman was rewarded with 2s 4d for holding the feast "comitabill for Thomas Carrow". It is not clear why the position of feastmaker should be so unpopular, but it is likely to be linked with the possible involvement of some financial commitment on behalf of the office holder. Such lack of enthusiasm did not prevent the feast from taking place regularly, with entertainment provided by Thomas Bylawe, the town minstrel, himself a member of the gild. It was held in the gild hall in Damgate, thought to be the building now numbered 29 and 31, and was certainly an occasion when the highly-valued gild pewter and special furniture were used.

The houses in Damgate today which were originally the hall of the Gild of All Saints

Indeed, the acquisition, preservation, and "renting out" of its pewter utensils became an important feature in the life of this gild, especially during the 1520s and 1530s. In 1509 a full inventory of the utensils of the gild was made, including those donated by various members. It comprised:-

"2 tables (one given by John Swete)
2 formes
2 stoles
1 cauldron (given by John Baxter)
1 brasspott (given by John Skinner)
12 plates of pewter
25 dishes of pewter
17 cowsters
1 forme (given by John Tynwhyte)
1 candelstyk (given by Agnes Seman)
1 laten bassen and a candylstyk (given by William Levald)"

A salt cellar   *"1 newe salt with a lydd"*

A candlestick and a latten basin

As we can see, several of these items were initially donated by members and this willingness to donate articles of some value was a recurring feature in the history of the gild For example, in 1506 Robert Newman had promised to bequeath all his "spetes and salerus" to the gild after his decease. The first income from the letting of the pewter was recorded as 7½d in 1516 and 4 years later John Kensey and John Machyn were given 7s 4d for the purchase of additional pewter articles. By 1522, after injection of a further 4s 8d, the additional stock included:-

"35 plates of pewter
35 dysches
2 raks to roste with
2 long spetes
1 newe salt with a lydd
10 newe saltes without a cover
2 new spetes of iron"

A spit in use

In 1525 a large sum of 19s 9d was paid out for an additional garnish of pewter, a set of vessels for use at the table. Two further spits were purchased in 1526, and over the next two years the gild was sufficiently solvent to purchase 11 new salts and a second garnish of pewter from Hewe Leveriche for 23s, as well as have the great "chettel" repaired. These utensils soon became the envy of other gilds, who were anxious to borrow items for celebrating their own feasts. The income generated by the letting of items rose from 12½d in 1523 to an average of 4s per annum in subsequent years, with a high peak of 5s 1d in 1529. Such was the importance of this activity to the gild that the two collectors of the alms money were now dubbed "keeper of the utensils" as well. It was their duty to make an annual check of all the pewter and replace any items that were missing. In 1530 it was necessary to spend 4d "in replacing of 1 pewter salter lost".

Unlike many of its contemporaries, the Gild of All Saints had no regular income of any size, which was to prove a contributory factor to its downfall. So much energy was expended in the letting of pewter that little attention was paid to the money-making activities popular amongst other Wymondham gilds, such as the employment of gild stock for interest. The Gild of All Saints preferred to spend its resources on the acquisition of pewter rather than loan sums of money to members. In fact only six are recorded as borrowing gild stock. It was just as well that gild finances were not solely dependent on the interest from these few loans, since the payments appear to have been made very spasmodically. This must have proved doubly annoying for John Machyn, the account maker. In addition to a decrease in income, he was forced to leave tell-tale gaps in his carefully-prepared financial statements. Of the few loans which had been made, some were repaid as early as 1512, and after 1513 all stock payments ceased to be recorded.

In view of this, how did the gild generate sufficient income for it to operate? The contributions made by newcomers certainly proved a useful source. The ingress fee varied between 12d and 20d, but the alternative method of payment on entry, organising a drinking, was very popular. This was done by the new members in groups of two or three, including wives, and was not limited to one per year, as in some other gilds. In 1506 there were three, and in 1519 four. Although of obvious enjoyment to members, these drinkings were more important for the revenue they provided, and in both of these years, made more than half of the total income.

The Gild of All Saints also differed from its counterparts in the ownership of land and properties. Its possessions were very limited and consequently provided little income. Throughout the period 1501 to 1536 only one property is referred to in the account book. Between 1501 and 1509 this was described as a house, which produced a constant annual rent of 2s 8d per annum. After the traumatic events of 1510, when there was no set of accounts, the rent had mysteriously jumped to 13s 4d the following year, and was then described as the gild hall. Considerable building work was undertaken on this property in 1512. Thomas Foster was employed to take down "the old house" and various workmen were employed for several weeks assembling, building and thatching "the newe house". Many of these were boarded by the tenant, John Colyour, who also donated certain items, such as "copylls, sparres and timber", to the construction. Reed rather than straw was used for the thatching, but roofing tiles were also purchased. This building work was not only extensive but it also revealed some degree of specialisation. Thomas Dowsing was responsible for taking out the old timber, while "Newman of Thorpe", a carpenter, assembled the new timber frame on the groundsill already fixed into place by William Bale. William Levald provided three loads of stone and Robert Wyseman constructed the groundsill's end. It took Richard Alden ten days to thatch the new house with the assistance of Richard Belman for eight and a half of them. Katheryn Tryman, the only female servant named in the accounts, was paid 3d for three days spent "drawyng thakk". John Colyour continued to be the tenant and lived in part of the building, which he eventually purchased before he died.

Obviously such an extensive programme of building came with a cost, and at the end of that year there was a difference of 34s 7d between income and expenditure, which alderman James Frosdyk was called upon to cover. The rent of the property remained at 13s 4d, which may have been in recognition of the varied gifts donated by the tenant, John Colyour, as well as the fact that he boarded many of the workers. Gild fortunes improved the following year and James Frosdyk was able to recoup his losses when receipts exceeded expenditure. In 1514 the gild acknowledged the improvements in their property, and in the accounts for that year and subsequent years referred to it as a mansion. One year later, the rent doubled to 26s 8d when further improvements were made. A wall had to be taken down and rebuilt with timber and clay, and Robert Grond and his servant constructed a pentis (a type of outhouse) on one side. Other work was carried out on the well, gates, stable, stairs, hearth and oven. The hole in the chamber wall was plugged and the backhouse wall strengthened. John Fischpole was paid to plaster, whiten and redden the hall, and buy additional supplies of red ochre. However, thatching, including the clearing up necessary afterwards, continued to be the biggest expense. On one occasion John Galle was paid for "beryng owt the mukk made by the thakters", and on another a man was paid to make clean the gutter "defild with the thaxter of John Dyn". An additional labourer was employed once or twice a year to "carry away the filth of the street".

In spite of the strain on the gild's resources made by such an extensive building programme, years of surplus of income over expenditure meant that there were still sufficient funds to cope with the usual gild financial commitments during this period, without having to rely on the alderman's support. Small sums were paid to the "brothers of Choseley", the guardians of the leper hospital at Westwade, and William Knyvett, the lord of the manor, for rent, and 20d was paid annually to maintain the light of All Saints in the parish church. The vicar received 4s each year for the certification of the gild, compulsory for all such organisations, and other priests were reimbursed for their special contributions to gild services.

Separate accounts were kept for the collection of alms money, which was usually made on the day of the annual dirge. These sums were used to pay for the obits of members when they died, and for the occasional charitable donation. The writers of the gild accounts usually received 8d per annum for their hard work. In 1503 it was Thomas Dobbys. Whether or not he was also responsible in 1512, when three attempts had to be made before the correct total of 47s 10d was calculated, we do not know.

The gild accounts finish in the year 1536, although the details are somewhat limited for the final year. Rather poignantly we can see that there was no income from the letting of the pewter vessels that year as they were "standing empty this year and so nothing received". With little other income, the situation was serious, and, even without government interference, it does not seem that the gild of All Saints could have lasted much longer. At the time of closure, the vicar John Drye had been alderman for seven years, and the decreasing income in the last few of these had left him with arrears of 34s 10d. It is not surprising that when he died a year later, his bequests to gilds did not extend to the Gild of All Saints. No doubt he felt that he had already given enough. The comparatively early demise of this gild gave members an opportunity to join others which were still flourishing. The Gild of St. John the Baptist welcomed Richard House and his wife Margaret, John Fedymont and Thomas Carrow, between the years 1541 and 1544. The treasured collection of pewter, along with that from other gilds, was probably passed to the churchwardens, who duly organised a "gatheryng of the pottes, panes, spetes and town pewter" during 1549.

The names of the brothers and sisters of the Gilde of All Saints in the year of our Lord 1502 and the year of the reign of King Henry Vll the 18th

Master Robt Irby vicar
Richard Denton and his wife
Robert Newman
William Blythe and his wife
Margery Denton
William Payn and his wife
Richard Payne and his wife
John Donthorne and his wife
John Curson and his wife
Peter Stanton and his wife
Harry Seman and his wife
Wiliam Perle and his wife
William Kyng and his wife
William Tetyssale and his wife
William Levald and his wife
William Wyseman
William Newlande and his wife
Agnes Newlande widow
John Sawer and his wife
Simon faml. Ric. Payn
William Smythe
Margaret Hynde
John Footeman and his wife
Robert Caly and his wife
Thomas Godfrey and his wife
Thomas Blythe and his wife
Gregory Galyon and his wife
Richard Martyn and his wife
Thomas Foster
Sir Thomas Dalys
John Davy and his wife
James Frosdyk and his wife
Thomas Walter and his wife
Richard Deynes and his wife

Thomas Spooner and his wife
Thomas Kedell
James Petyt and his wife
Thomas Jeffrey and his wife
Thomas Dobbys
Thomas Dowsing and his wife
Richard Caron and his wife
Harry Brown

1502
Willm Fedymont
John Tye and his wife
Willm Dowe
Simon Mannyng

1503
Johanna Curson

1504
Dom James Curson
Margaret Denton
Margaret Dobbys
Fryer Matthew

1505
William Garrerd
Thomas Carrow
Dom Thomas Gresham
Robert Roo
Matilda Chore

1507
John Colyor
Katherine his wife
Thomas Lowes
Agnes his wife
Katherine Dawe
Wife of Ric.Caron
Robert Ford and his wife

1508
John Kensy jun
John Galle
John Machyn
John Fedymont

1510
Dom Thomas Porter vicar
Brother William Horncreyk
Robert Plomer
Agnes wife of John Machyn
Alice wife of John Galle
John Whytechurche
John Kett

1511
Thomas Sendell and his wife
wife of Willm Fedymont
wife of John Colyor
wife of John Kensey
wife of John Whytechurch
Dom John Hengham
wife of Thomas Sponer
wife of Robert Fordin
Dom Thomas Esmund

1512
Robert Wyseman
John Godfery mason
Margaret Dynne
Thomas Bylawe

1513
John Swete

1514
John Drye vicar
Francis Coper and his wife
Wife of Richard Deynes
Richard Howse and his wife
wife of John Kett
wife of Thomas Bylawe
wife of Edmund Marchall
wife of John Tye

1516
Robert Wyseman jun
John Fysshepole
Richard Fedymont
John Randoll
Isabella Payne
Brother Robert Wyndhows

1517
wife of Richard Fedymont
wife of Robert Wyseman jun
wife of John Fysshepole
Isabella Payne

1518
William Rowse
and his wife
Thomas Petytt and his wife
Rose Foster widow
Agnes Archerd wid
Dom Flowerdew
Brother August
Brother Robert Kyng
Dom Robert Frosdyk

1519
Avice Kytmay
Margaret Anngell
John Godfrey glover
Willm Kyng
Wife of Robt Wyseman
Margaret Bylawe

1520
Stephen Verdon

1521
Richard Deplage
John Randoll

1522
wife Deplage
Richard Potter
his wife

1524
Henry Dyman
His wife
Richard Kyddell

1525
John Garnett and Agnes his wife
Margaret Keddell wife of
Richard Keddell

1526
Dom John Sygar priest
Thomas Elyngham
Catherine his wife
John Dawe
Simon Sallett
Margaret Stephynson

1527
Margaret Kynge
Agnes Salett

1528
Alexander Jeffrey
Thomas Dynes

1530
Robt Crashfeld
Jo his wife
Cristina Kydell wife of
Richard Kydell
Isabella Deynes
Isabella Brown wife of
Thomas Brown
Wife Rows Lydya

1531
Thomas Brown sherman
Isabella his wife

1532
Thomas Kett
Sibilla Sendell
Elizabeth Ponyante widow
John Cheeseman
John Sewe

THE GILD OF HOLY TRINITY

Members of the gild of the Holy Trinity met in their gildhall in Spooner Row, and as a result this gild was often referred to as the Spooner Row gild. Membership, however, was not restricted to residents of this community alone, and brothers and sisters travelled from Wymondham as well as from the neighborouring parishes of Besthorpe and Morley, to join other members from Wattlefield and Suton. No official list of members of the gild of the Holy Trinity for the early part of sixteenth century exists, but we are able to discover the names of many of them from bequests in their wills and from the gild's account book, which covered the period 1517 to 1545, from which we can follow the payment or non-payment of the annual interest due on their holdings of gild stock, and note the names of the new entrants which are given for some years. All the indications are that this gild was of a size comparable to that of the other gilds in Wymondham at this time, and their hall, built in 1460, probably on the site of the present chapel-of-ease in Spooner Row, was large enough to accommodate them.

The chapel at Spooner Row, dedicated to the Holy Trinity, which stands on the probable site of the Gild Hall

The Bede Roll of 1524 contains reference to an image of the Trinity, given by Thomas Westgate, and established in the choir of the parish church. William Lombe and Robert Dyn provided a tabernacle to house it, which was gilded by John Kensey. The Dyn family had close associations with this gild, and for eighteen years John Dyn, possibly Robert's brother, was its alderman. During this time he stood "pledge" or surety for up to six fellow members. We have seen such action was not without its risks, as John discovered to his cost, when, in 1531, on the death of Richard Martyn, he had to repay his debt of 6s 8d. As well as the usual officials, two butlers and a beadle were appointed. In addition to organising the drinkings, such an important source of gild revenue, butlers were resposible for maintaining the light before the image of the Holy Trinity in the parish church, buying furniture and pewter, and the letting of the latter to supplement gild funds, which, although important, was not on the same scale as the Gild of All Saints. The beadle had to attend all requiem masses held for the late founders and benefactors, supervise repairs to gild properties and collect the rents. For these tasks he was paid an annual sum of 2d "in reward".

The account book confirms the sound financial position of the Gild of the Holy Trinity, which was an unusual situation in Wymondham. It was the only gild with existing records in which the annual income always exceeded the annual expenses. Astute handling of the profits each year consolidated this position and saw most of them being re-issued as gild stock for interest. Lengthy discussions took place among the Election as to what should be done with any monies still remaining, and in 1520 it was decided that they should be placed in a "coffyr", ready to defray any further expenses that year. Five years later this receptacle was described as the "comon chyst".

How did this sound financial situation come about? Much of it was due to the income received from the interest on the gild stock loaned to members. This sum varied from year to year, but averaged about £2 annually. The interest was paid regularly at the beginning of our period by all members, but by the 1530s it was becoming less so, and there is evidence of many defaulters. John Sygar appears to have paid no interest at all on his loan of 3s 4d for twenty years, between 1517 and 1537, but the worst offender for non-payment was Thomas Lombe, gentleman, who was the Alderman from 1517 to

1519 and again later. When the form of the presentation of the accounts changed during the period of John Dyn's leadership, it was revealed that Thomas Lombe had borrowed three sums of 5s, 20s, and 16s 8d, but had made no interest payments at all on them for over ten years. In spite of this, however, he continued to act as surety for six other members, and the Election seem to have accepted the situation, as there were no official pronouncements or threats to non-paying members, common to other gilds. Again there may have been an accepted reason for Thomas Lombe's lack of interest charges, which is not revealed in the account book, perhaps involving the rental of land to the gild. It was not always easy for members to find guarantors for their loans, which is not surprising, but much family support was given in this situation. Richard Baxter stood surety for his brother Robert, and Richard Brown acted in the same capacity for his brother, another Robert. The same arrangement occurred between the brothers Richard and Robert Howse. These Christian names were obviously very popular at the time. Fathers too did their duty, and often supported sons when they took gild loans for the first time. Thomas Luce acted for his son Thomas, and John Colman for his son John. This practice of giving the eldest, usually the eldest, son his father's name was quite common, and causes considerable confusion to the present-day reader of records. Sometimes the words senior or junior are added to the name which can be helpful at times, but eventually a "junior" becomes"'senior", and more problems ensue. Where the family was unable, or unwilling, to act as guarantors, ties of friendship were often used, and in a gesture of mutual support members stood surety for each other. Stephen Woodcock and Robert Colman senior came to such an arrangement in 1517 and this proved satisfactory to both. Stephen Woodcock also stood as surety to another friend, Stephen Potter, but with a less happy outcome. He was faced with a massive bill of 36s 8d when Stephen Potter died in 1529, and it took him three years to pay off the debt.

In addition to the monies received from loans at the usual rate, there was a regular income from the letting of gild properties. In comparison with other gilds, these were relatively few, only three in fact, which included just a single cottage. A positive advantage of this situation was that the gild did not have to expend great sums on the maintenance and repairs to buildings, which, as we have seen, drained the resources of others. This was just as well, since the cottage was in Spooner Row and practically all the materials needed for repair had to be carried from Wymondham, adding considerably to the total cost. In fact there are only four references to major repairs on the property in the gild account book. The kitchen floor was refitted in 1521, using 300 feet of borde supplied by William Bale and five pieces of timber bought from John Dyn. John Agas was paid 4d for "carryng the borde from town". As a result of these improvements, the rent from the cottage rose from 2s 4d to 5s per annum and remained at this level until the end of the accounts in 1545. The impoverished Richard Martyn, whom we have already met, was the tenant of the cottage from 1521 to 1531, and in this respect managed to pay his rent regularly. Thomas Lombe, alderman in 1525, was faced with a repair bill of 26s 4d that year, but there is no breakdown of the expenditure. The inevitable need for the re-thatching of the gild property arose in 1530 and cost 17s 4d. Thomas Hempsale, who thatched properties for the Gilds of St. John the Baptist and All Saints in the same year, was employed to carry out the work with the help of two labourers. The broches and bindings used in the operation were obtained locally. Four years later the thatch needed further attention and this time Robert Craschfeld was called in. He was assisted by Thomas Colyour, a member of the gild, who provided the broches and bindings.

A sizeable meadow, held of the manor of Grishaugh, was let for another annual sum of 5s. It was usually tenanted by two, and on some occasions three people, and was obviously very popular among the members, who vied for its tenancy. As with all major gild policy matters, it was the Election who was left to make the final decision. Little maintenance was needed on the meadow, and the only outlay required was that for repairs to the road leading to it. A beneficial sideline was the additional income generated from the sale of wood from it, which amounted to 6s in 1522. The only other regular property "let" was that of one and a half acres of arable land, which brought in 12d per annum, and was let to Robert Colman senior from 1529 until 1535.

The total wealth of the gild enabled it to acquire considerable amounts of furniture and pewter. Befitting his important position, the alderman was supplied with a chair at meetings, even though it needed replacing from time to time.

Other members had to be satisfied with the usual benches or forms, and the gild possessed sufficient of these to seat all at the gild feast. Fortunately there is enough evidence available from existing records to enable us to picture this very important annual event in the gild calendar. The room was arranged with a high table at one end and others radiating from it. All of these would be covered with table cloths, and on them would be a trencher and spoon for everyone. The purchase of "a grosse of trenchores and 10 dosen spones" in 1535 gives us a clear estimate of the average attendance at this gathering.

A trencher, pewter plate and spoon can be seen in this sketch. Wymondham was not only famous for its spoons at this time, wood-turning was also a major industry in the town.

Candlesticks painted in gold and "othyr colers" also adorned the tables and the gild's supply of pewter salts and garnishes completed the decorations. The Holy Trinity was another gild which was proud of its collection of pewter, repairing items when necessary, and adding to them whenever possible. Such items did not come cheaply, and in the early 1520s they were forced to pay 12s 6d for a garnish of pewter and 20s for 40lbs of pewter "ready wrought". Some of their outlay was recovered from the proceeds of hiring out these items to other gilds, for their feasts, but this did not produce as much income as the gild of All Saints. In 1533 it raised 2s 6d.

So much for the table arrangements, but what was actually eaten? The election decided, and informed the feastmakers what they were to provide in no uncertain terms. On the Gild Sunday, it had to be potage, "hoole gosse and veale, pygge, moton and custard", presumably not all at the same time. On the following day the fare was to be the same, except that the brothers and sisters had to be content with only half a goose. It also appears that this gild had celebration meals on two consecutive days. For these treats each member had the privilege of paying 6d, which was collected by the feast makers on the Monday. The meal was completed with the usual treat of entertainment by one or two of the town's minstrels, referred to as "Andrew, Strowger or Barbar", and occasionally by a small band of players.

The Election of the Gild of the Holy Trinity was particularly powerful and its edicts were not solely confined to the field of food. In 1523 the gild banner, used on all ceremonial occasions, needed replacing and Robert Flory was appointed to make a new one. He was told in no uncertain terms by the Election that the replacement should be exactly the same as the old "in every condycion". The agreed price was 53s 4d, which was quite a large sum when compared to rents and wages at this time. The gild paid 10s down, but was adamant that no further money would be forthcoming until the "baner be full fenyshed".

It was able to spend such sums on a replacement banner because its regular outgoings were comparatively few. We have already seen that repairs to property were much less than in other gilds. As one would expect of a religious brotherhood, alms were given regularly to the poor and sick, and sometimes distributed in the churchyard at Wymondham. These sums were given from a fund collected for that specific purpose, and therefore not a financial drain on the general gild account. Two members, appointed annually for this purpose, raised an average of between 8s and 9s every year. Other regular beneficiaries of the Holy Trinity's generosity. were the four orders of friars in Norwich.

Three families dominated the activities of the gild at this time.

One of them was the family of William Brown and his five sons, Stephen, Richard, Robert, Thomas and John. The only one not to make any contribution to the Gild of the Holy Trinity was John, who lived at Griston. Stephen, who was probably the eldest, was a landowner of considerable means, with properties in Suton, Wattlefield and Besthorpe as well as in Spooner Row itself, where he lived. The road between Spooner Row and Wymondham was well-used, and like many roads at this time it was in constant need of repair. Conscious of this, Stephen Brown left 13s 4d in his will of 1536 for "the mendyng and reparyng of the hye waye betwene trynyte gyldhows in Sponerow until hamstede gate in Wymondham". As a sheep rearer and producer of barley and beet, he would have used it often to transport his produce to market. After a brief period as a feastmaker and butler for the gild, Stephen Brown became a member of the Election and served on it, almost continuously, from 1517 until 1531. He set his fellow members a very good example by paying the interest on his gild stock with great regularity and never defaulted. On his death, Stephen requested that he should be buried in the churchyard at Wymondham, and made a bequest of 20d to the church. This sum, however, was much less than the 6s 8d he left for repairs to the church at Tacolneston, where other members of the extended Brown family lived.

Important contributions were also made by Robert and Richard Brown over an even longer period of time, covering twenty-one years. Although they served a much shorter time on the Election, they acted as surety for each other and fulfilled the roles of feastmaker, butler and beadle at various times. Both Robert and his wife were employed by the gild in 1517, when he repaired some palings to gild properties. We are not told the nature of her work, but she became a member the following year. Thomas Brown, another brother, lived in Morley, and held some minor offices in the gild. In 1531 he was joined by William Pakk, the rector of Morley, who was appointed feastmaker that year. No doubt both of them also belonged to the Gild of St. Botolph, which met in the village of Morley at this time.

The Colman family, who farmed land in Suton and Spooner Row, was also well-represented among gild officials and played an active part in its life. Contemporary documents are once again difficult to interpret regarding this family because there were both senior and junior members of the family called Robert, Richard, Thomas and John, who were all members of the gild at the same time. Writers of the gild accounts were not always consistent with the spelling of surnames, and, as we have seen, often forgot to distinguish between father and son with the same name. Roberts senior and junior held minor offices, and Robert junior rented gild property. John senior was an alms collector and served as a member of the Election for eighteen years, eight of which were at the same time as his son John.

A total of eight members of the Wodecock family were also members of the Gild of the Holy Trinity, and again we have a problem with names. There was William senior and junior, John senior and junior, Robert and his wife, Agnes, Richard and Stephen. Once again, the family does not appear to have belonged to any other gild, which suggests they lived in or near Spooner Row. Stephen Wodecock was the most active of them. In addition to borrowing small sums of gild stock himself, he stood surety for six of his fellow members, one of whom, Stephen Potter, cost him dearly, as we have already seen. Stephen Wodecock was another long-serving member of the Election for eighteen years.

The last year in which full accounts were made was 1538. These were followed by brief entries for 1539 and 1544. The gild was still functioning in 1542, when John Nevel made his will, but he was obviously uncertain as to the gild's future at this stage, as he left a bequest of 3s 4d to the gild of the Holy Trinity "if it be styll kept". It certainly lasted long enough to benefit from this gift, when John Nevel died the following year.

THE GILD OF OUR LADY'S LIGHT

In many ways the 'gild' of Our Lady's Light differed from the other Wymondham gilds. In fact it was not really a gild at all in the contemporary use of the term. For reasons we shall discover later, it would be more accurate to refer to the organisation as a fraternity rather than a gild. In making such a decision we are supported by the views of the members themselves, since the term "gild" was used only twice in our main source of evidence, the account book. The term fraternity is used slightly more often, and this would seem to be a more accurate description of the key elements in the lives of the members of the society of Our Lady's Light. The accounts themselves are defined in the records as those of the "colyours" (collectors) of Our Lady's Light in the chapel in the north aisle, and the principal aim seems to have been the maintenance of this light, and the provision of torches and other lights for funeral services and processions. Very shrewd economic thinking and planning lay behind the activities of this fraternity, with less attention being given to the prayer and philanthropy more common in the gilds. Indeed it has been suggested by H. L. Hayward in his article in "The Builder" in 1923, that fraternities such as Our Lady's Light were the forerunners of our present day freemasonry organisations.

As we have seen, our main source of evidence for the practices and proceedings of "Our Lady's Light" is the account book dated 1506 to 1540. Perhaps it would be more accurate to say the pages of the account book which are left. The period 1506 to 1527 is fully covered, but the accounts for the year 1527 are followed by those for 1536/7, and the pages after this year are somewhat disorganised and add little to our knowledge. What happened to the intervening pages is something of a mystery. Or is it? Is it a coincidence that in the 1884 issue of Norfolk Archaeology G. R. Carthew made a summary of the accounts for these intervening years? He also included a transcription of the rules of the society which is another document now missing from the muniment room of the Abbey. In spite of these limitations, however, we are still able to get a fairly clear picture of what happened in the life of the fraternity during the early years of the sixteenth century. A superficial glance at the accounts is sufficient to see the emphasis the fraternity placed on the borrowing of its common stock and the collection of the interest accrued on it.

Many of the fraternity's rules were the same as those of the gilds. All members were expected to be loyal to the organisation and obey its regulations without question. Office holding was considered to be an important element in the society, and, if elected, a member could not decline the honour without being liable to the customary fine of four pounds of wax, or being made responsible for the assessment of the profits of the stock. The usual requirements to attend requiem mass on the death of a fellow member was rigidly enforced, as were those restraining members from challenging their fellows in court, without firstly bringing the issue to the attention of the fraternity's officials for settlement. The position of alderman did not exist in the fraternity of Our Lady's Light, and the overall leadership was spread between the collectors chosen by the twelve electors. At the beginning of the century they were four in number, but by 1522 had reduced to three, only to become four again in 1527. Other key appointments included someone to provide and replenish the torches, which seemed to involve considerable time and expense, and featured highly in the list of offices of the society. A beadle was also elected annually, but does not appear to have been of sufficient significance to record every year. Perhaps the most important difference, however, between the fraternity of Our Lady's Light and the religious gilds in Wymondham, was that it did not celebrate an annual feast with the usual merriment and entertainment. The provision of food and drink is rarely mentioned in the account book, apart from the few occasions when John and Agnes Mayden fed the scribe as he prepared the annual accounts.

In 1889, G. A. Carthew made an analysis of the list of members from a document, which has since been lost - another of those he forgot to return? Unfortunately we are not able to identify many individuals, but we are told that the list contained one hundred and twenty-four names, and was headed by the vicar, John Drye, and the chaplain, Robert Neyling. This number could be somewhat misleading, as we know from the lists to which we do have access that they were usually continuous, with yearly additions, and there could well have been considerably fewer than this number of active members in any one year. Of those recorded, we read that twenty-two were wives, and a further eighteen were females, the latter probably being widows, since there is no evidence to suggest that single women were eligible to join.

Election Day was the Sunday following Whit Sunday, when officers were chosen, and members were required to pay all their dues and interest charges, and bring their borrowed stock and chattels to the meeting, as laid down in the rules. On this occasion the year's accounts were presented, and an up-to-date list of stockholders was published. In 1506, fifty-four members were recorded to have borrowed sums totalling £24 18s 8d, ranging from Thomas Carr's 8d at one end of the scale to Richard Dyman's 34s 4d at the other. The average amount borrowed was about 5s. All debtors were asked to provide a guarantor when their loans were arranged, and members usually acted for each other in this capacity. Interest was charged at the usual flat rate of 10% and collected annually, together with any repayments of the original loan which could be afforded. Occasionally the debt would be cleared in one transaction, but more usually it took a few years to pay off. Prompt payments were positively encouraged, but not always achieved, and in 1508 the Election felt that it was necessary to decree that any member failing to pay in time would be subjected to a fine of 1lb of wax. This was not always sufficient encouragement for prompt payment, and the fraternity were forced to stipulate a planned programme of repayments for Richard Dyman's large loan, referred to above. He was to repay 3s 4d on ten special feast days, such as All Saints, Candlemas, Lammas, and Hallowmas, and the vicar and Robert Sterling were official witnesses to this arrangement. Loans still outstanding at the time of death were settled promptly by a legacy, if there was one left for that purpose. If not, the family of the deceased would attempt to do so, usually over a period of years. Failing that, however, the debt was left the full responsibility of the unfortunate gild member who had agreed to "stand pledge". Examples of these arrangements can be seen in 1508, when John Mayden paid 3s 4d in full payment of his father's debt, and two years later John Plomer's debt of 30s was paid by his executors. Gradually, however, over the period of the account book, the fraternity changed its policy of offering money for interest, and, in the absence of more than one piece of land possessed for renting, turned its attention to the purchase of animals, which could be offered to members for loan.

The concept of renting single animals may seem rather strange to us today, but although it appears to have been the only organisation under our present review which engaged in this practice, it was quite common in the early sixteenth century, when the price of a single cow was well beyond the means of many. This policy began in 1520 when Thomas Sendell purchase two cows for 18s 4d, which represented the surplus from the previous year's accounts, and proceeded to rent them for 3s 4d per annum until 1527. In 1523 two "milch neats" were bought at Pulham Fair for 16s 8d, and on another occasion the collectors were allocated the sum of 44s to purchase four more "milch neats before Candelmass". The purchase of animals, usually at the cost of approximately 10s a head, continued throughout the intervening years, and John Kett was a regular renter of some of them. Robert Vekere joined the scheme in 1526, when he paid 22d for the rent of one cow for that year. Robert Sterling appeared to have had a bargain when he was charged only 8d for one year's "ferme" of a cow, but it must have been of inferior quality as it was sold a year later for 11s to John Kett, who was a member of the fraternity and a butcher, but also related to Robert Kett, who was to become such an important figure in the history of Wymondham. Some animals changed hands annually whilst others remained with the same person much longer. This arrangement was a very useful introduction to animal husbandry, and John Neve's experience was so successful that he purchased his two neats after renting them for a year. Other cows were sold from time to time, usually at the end of their milk-producing years, to butchers, although sometimes the carcass was divided before sale. In the 1534/1535 accounts we read of 14d being paid for the "skyn of cowe ded", and in 1536, 2s was paid for the "hyde of a cowe in the ferme of John Poll".

The only opportunity for social engagement among the members of "Our Lady's Light" was the occasion of a gild drinking, which also provided a very useful source of income. These occasions started in 1516 with a single "drinking", made at the home of John Mayden, one of the colyours, who kept an alehouse, and who often provided refreshments when the annual accounts were being prepared. He and his wife also "boarded" workmen who came into the town when specialist advice was necessary. After 1520, new entrants were expected to organise drinkings when joining the fraternity, sometimes as an alternative to paying the usual ingress money. They did not, however, have to foot the bill, as the rules stipulated that each member should contribute 1d towards the cost. In another move to keep expenses as low as possible, members gave combs of malt for brewing when they entered the gild, in preparation for such events, and a list of these donors is recorded on a loose sheet at the back of the account book, where Thomas Bothom is recorded as failing to fulfil his obligation in this matter. Drinkings seem to have been particularly popular in 1530, when three took place, raising the sums of 7s, 9s 4d, and 9s respectively. The first was organised by Henry Dyman, Francis Gedney and Robert Wiseman, the second by Robert Mechell, John Sygar and William Moore, and the third by John Bale and his wife, and Robert Elyott and his wife.

Always ready to maximise its income, the members of the fraternity of Our Lady's Light sometimes turned to the people of Wymondham for a contribution to their funds, when they made a "gathering" or collection within the town, usually as part of their procession on one of the many feast days in the church calendar. These gatherings, an example of which is used for the cover design, and repeated below, proved quite lucrative, and two such events held in 1516, brought in 20s and 24s 2d for the general fund. Very little of this was donated to charitable causes.

People of Wymondham contributing to the funds of the fraternity of Our Lady's Light

This fraternity was well managed and became very prosperous. Year after year, the accounts showed a healthy surplus, which was often invested in the purchase of further stock. Further evidence of this prosperity was the fraternity's ability to maintain its own chaplain, and for some time Robert Neylyng was paid a stipend of 26s 8d per quarter for this office. Other religious gilds had to rely on the services of the lesser clergy, who were, in most cases, members of that particular gild. The chaplain of "Our Lady's Light" was responsible for overseeing its religious activities, which, as we have seen, were centred in the "chapel in the north aisle". Here, a considerable amount of its income was spent on wax, and on maintaining the light in front of the image of the Virgin Mary. Torches also played an important part in processions and celebrations, and even greater sums were expended on the provision of these. The official responsible for their replenishment was paid 4d per annum for his pains. The total sum spent on torches and lights varied each year, but in 1505 it was over 10s, indicating that there must have an exceptional number of spectacular processions that year.

No reference is made to a meeting hall in the accounts of the brethren of our Lady's Light, and it would appear that all their more formal meetings were held in the north aisle of the parish church. Two factors suggest this. Firstly, there is a conspicuous absence of any reference to repairs and maintenance of a separate hall, and there would have been many if one had existed, and, secondly, in 1511 the gild was financially responsible for the repair of a window in the north aisle. If it had ever possessed a separate meeting hall, it was no longer large enough to use, but since there was no annual feast there was little point in wasting money maintaining one. It made economic sense to hire a gild hall for the few occasions during the year when the fraternity held its drinkings.

The repair of the window in the north aisle was quite expensive, and we have detailed, first-hand evidence of its progress. First of all, John Jobson had to be paid 7d to remove the old window, and then the costly process of transporting stone to the town began. Much of this came overland from Brandon Ferry, where it had arrived by river, and it is worth noting that the carriage of the stone cost four times the purchase price. Naturally, the expenses of the new window did not stop there. The sum of thirty shillings was paid to the masons for setting up the new stone framework, and then Thomas Cheeseman was commissioned to make a wooden replica of it, which could be used by the glaziers as a pattern for their work. Another 34s 2d had to be found on completion of the glazing.

In the early 1500s nine of the eleven windows in the north aisle were altered. The fraternity of Our Lady's Light was one donor

A year later, in 1512, the fraternity was involved in further outlay, and embarked upon another, much more ambitious project in the town. The plan was to set up a stone cross in the churchyard, following the pattern of similar constructions elsewhere. Its purpose was to sanctify the churchyard as well as to contribute to the Easter processions. On Palm Sunday it was used as the second of the processional stations of the cross, and the one at which the mass was celebrated. After the celebration, it was ceremoniously wreathed in "palms", which were usually branches of yew. A considerable amount of effort was involved in building such a structure, and in Wymondham the work, and more importantly, the cost, was spread over more than one year. Stone crosses were usually placed on a stepped base, and included a small tabernacle, rather than a cross-head, with niches for the image of Christ, the Virgin, or the Saints with a vacant niche in readiness for the Host used for the Palm Sunday mass.

The account book of the fraternity of Our Lady's Light gives us an insight into the various stages of the construction. The first task was to commission Richard "Ylward", a freemason from Norwich, to come and inspect the site, in preparation for the initial groundwork. This is probably a reference to Richard Elward, who worked in Norwich and Beccles, and whose name appears in several Norwich documents of this period. The following year saw the arrival of large supplies of stone in the town, and Richard Elward and his servant made two trips to Yarmouth, presumably to organise collection of the special stone which had arrived by sea. A further ton of special stone, together with a greater amount of freestone, was once again collected from Brandon Ferry, and additional supplies of freestone as well as sand and lime were obtained from local sources. The stone arriving at Brandon was probably of superior quality to that collected at Yarmouth, and more suited to the elaborate carvings which were planned. In all this work, Elward was assisted by local masons John Bylaw and Roger Woodecocke, who had also helped to transport the stone. He then supervised the construction of the shaft of the cross, which was brought to the town by Thomas Sendell.

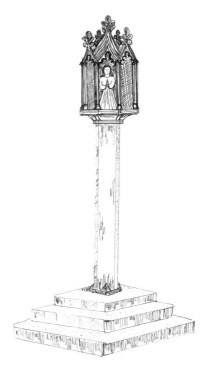

Artist's impression of the Wymondham Churchyard Cross, before the addition of the twelve apostles.

Little progress appears to have been made in 1514, although the accounts reveal a surplus of funds, but during the following year a special stone was transported to New Buckenham. This is exactly the time when the lavish south aisle of the church there was under construction by a team of masons from away, who specialised in elaborate carvings, and would suggest that the churchyard cross in Wymondham was beautifully carved and very special. Some of the stonemasons and carvers were boarded in the town, including "Thomas the mason", who seems to have been the principal one, earning 6d per day. The Wymondham cross was then primed and thatched to protect it from the weather. All expenses involved in the construction of the cross are carefully recorded by the writer of the fraternity's accounts. The annotation at the side of each entry allowed him to calculate, in 1516, that the "holle coste of the qwech haff be don from the fowdacion of the crosse on tylle the fulle making of the seid crosse ys £11 7s 11d". It does not appear to have been the final cost, however, and after five years carved figures of the twelve apostles were made, painted, and then attached, completing what must have been a very fine and unique addition to the churchyard in Wymondham.

The generous donation of the stone cross, coupled with the gift of the window in the north aisle, earned the fraternity a great deal of gratitude from the church and parishioners, the result of which was its inclusion in the list of benefactors of the church made in 1524, which earned it the prayers of the Wymondham faithful.

The activities of the fraternity of Our Lady's Light continued after the demise of many of the Wymondham gilds. The last account recorded is for 1539/40 when it arranged two drinkings and still possessed seven cows. Membership continued to be strong, and fourteen members, including Robert Kett, were selected for the Election that year. By this time the interest on loans seems to have dwindled to nothing, and income was derived mainly from drinkings, ingress money, and the renting of cows. The last bequests were made in 1538 by Rose Seman, the widow of Stephen, and by Agnes Cotyngham.

Collectors of the "stokke of the lyte of our Blyssyd Lady Mary of Wymondham"

1505	John Plomer	Robt Sterling	John Hed	Robt Symonds
1506	John Plomer	Robt Sterling	Willm Lewald	Robt Symonds
1507	John Plomer	Robt Sterling	Willm Lewald	Robt Symonds
1508	WillmTetysale	Robt Sterling	Willm Lewald	Robt Symonds
1509				
1510	WillmTetysale	Robt Sterling	Willm Lewald	Robt Symonds
1511	WillmTetysale	Robt Sterling	Willm Lewald	Robt Symonds
1512	WillmTetysale	John Maydon	Willm Lewald	Thoms Sendell
1513	WillmTetysale	John Maydon	Willm Lewald	Thoms Sendell
1514	WillmTetysale	John Maydon	Willm Lewald	Thoms Sendell
1515	WillmTetysale	John Maydon	Willm Lewald	Thoms Sendell
1516	WillmTetysale	John Maydon	Willm Lewald	Thoms Sendell
1517	WillmTetysale	John Maydon	Willm Lewald	Thoms Sendell
1518	WillmTetysale	John Maydon	Willm Lewald	Thoms Sendell
1519	WillmTetysale	John Gay	Robert Dey	Thoms Sendell
1520	WillmTetysale	John Gay	Robert Dey	Thoms Sendell
1521	WillmTetysale	John Gay	Robert Dey	Thoms Sendell
1522	Adam Bishop	John Joby		Thoms Sendell
1523	Adam Bishop	John Joby		Thoms Sendell
1524	Adam Bishop	John Joby		Thoms Sendell
1525	Adam Bishop	John Symonds		Thoms Sendell
1526	Adam Bishop	John Symonds		Thoms Sendell
1527	Adam Bishop	John Symonds	John Kensey ju	Thoms Sendell
1528	FrancsGedney	WillmKett	John Kensey ju	Thoms Sendell
1529	FrancsGedney	WillmKett	John Kensey ju	Thoms Sendell
1530	FrancsGedney	WillmKett	Robert Elyott	Thoms Sendell
1531	Thomas Petyt	HenryDyman	Robert Elyott	Thoms Sendell
1532	Thomas Petyt	HenryDyman	Robert Elyott	Thoms Sendell
1533	AdamBishop	JohnSymonds	John Dyn	Thoms Sendell
1534	AdamBishop	JohnSymonds	John Dyn	Thoms Sendell

The mid-fifteenth century north porch of Wymondham Abbey has references to the Virgin Mary and Saint Thomas to whom the Abbey is dedicated. Above the doorway Ms on the left and Ts on the right probably suggest that one of the niches contained a statue of Our Lady and the other one of St. Thomas, which would be highly valued by their gilds.

OTHER GILDS

The Gild of Saint Thomas

The Gild of St. Thomas in Wymondham was the earliest known fraternity in the country to be dedicated to that saint. It was founded in 1187, fourteen years after the canonization of Thomas à Becket, and sometimes referred to as the Middleton Gild or the Wattlefield Gild. The use of the former name derives from the position of the gild chapel and hall in that area of the town. The reference to Wattlefield is less clear, and all previous studies have failed to give any reasons why it should have been so named.

Documentary evidence, particularly the wills, suggests that there could have been two branches of the same gild in the parish, one meeting in Middleton in the town, and another, much smaller, sometimes meeting at Wattlefield, possibly in a member's house. Bequests to the gilds always stipulated the place of meeting, in order to avoid confusion over gilds of the same name which met in adjoining parishes. Certainly we know that the gild of the Holy Trinity met in Spooner Row, and it is described as such by the testators. Thomas Kok's will clearly refers to the gilds of St Thomas the Martyr in Wattlefield, St. Margaret in Wymondham, St. Botolph in Morley and Our Blessed Lady in Wymondham, in addition to the Holy Trinity in "Sponerow".

He was not the only person to state that the gild met in Wattlefield. Six others do so as well, including three members of the Mannyng family. Certainly a branch meeting point at Wattlefield would be particularly helpful to members such as William Plomer who lived at Silfield, and would mean that some members did not always need to come into the town, apart from special occasions and processions. The theory of a branch of the Gild of St. Thomas meeting at Wattlefield from time to time seems more likely than that of a separate gild established there. However, wherever it was that the brothers and sisters met, there is no doubt that the gild, dedicated to the same patron as the Abbey Church, held a high profile within the parish, and during the early sixteenth century attracted the highest number of bequests of any gild.

A chapel dedicated to the murdered archbishop was founded in the centre of the town by William d'Albini's son as early as 1174, and this was a natural centre for all the religious activities of the gild, who maintained lights before the altar there.

The gild chapel of St. Thomas à Becket

Another gild to attract many of the wealthier inhabitants of the town, it built up the ownership of much property through bequests over the years. During the early sixteenth century, a total of 36 bequests were made, and, though not all of these involved property, sizeable sums of money were left by many. In 1519 William Symonds, father of priest John Symonds who features frequently in the activities of several gilds, left a cottage and a close to the Gild of St. Thomas. A wealthy man, who had lived in what he described himself as a mansion, he was of sufficient importance to be buried within the Abbey itself, rather than in the churchyard. The cottage bequeathed to the gild had previously belonged to Nicholas Reyner and was left without condition. The close, initially left to the younger son, Henry, was to pass at his death to the gild, provided that its members held a yearly obit for Henry's soul and the souls of his friends. William had already arranged a yearly obit for his own soul with a grant of 5s. His total possessions included several cottages and closes, together with pastures, meadows, and more than 35 acres of arable land.

A year later, another endowment was made by William Hale, otherwise known as Payne. He left 3s 4d to each of the gilds of St. Peter, All Saints, and the Holy Cross, but 6s 8d to the gild of St. Thomas, together with 20 loads of gravel, "out of my pitte at Wayrthill if they receve me as a brother and my wife as a sister". This is an interesting condition, and an example of only a few Wymondham testators joining a gild after death, in order to benefit from the prayers of its living members. The bequeathed gravel was to be used for the repairs to the gild chapel. William Hale, another of the more wealthy men of Wymondham at this time, was buried in the "holy sepulchre of the parish church".

These bequests represent only a small part of lands owned by the gild. One of the first, a messuage in Middleton, in a street called Flassegate, was in its ownership as early as 1328. In 1380, the gild had acquired another two pieces of arable land in Northfield, at a point called Tolys Cross. Another acre in the same field was added in 1408, but fifteen years later a small parcel of land and part of a tenement called Nelond was surrended to John Kempe, who owned the adjoining property. A rental of the gild lands in 1464, summarised by Carthew in 1889, lists all the properties in the gild's ownership at this time; it included four messuages, twenty-seven pieces of land of various types, and several houses, including two halls, identified as the old gildhall and the new gildhall. The total revenue that year was £13 18s 1½d. These extensive possessions required considerable attention, and two members were chosen annually by the gild to be responsible for the collection of the rents.

Acquisition of properties continued after 1464, and a title deed of 1507 indicate that two further tenements, called Boysts, with the old gild house, and Poleyns, with the new gild house, were purchased that year. The messuage called Poleyns (spelt differently in different documents), is worth special mention, as it appears quite often in the surviving Wymondham title deeds. Situated in Flassegate, adjoining the messuage already belonging to the gild of St. Thomas, it was named, following the usual custom, after a previous owner, or indeed owners. This particular property belonged to two Adam Poleyns. The first was the prior in Wymondham for seventeen years, who died on Christmas Day 1303. The messuage must then have passed to a relative, perhaps nephew, again called Adam Poleyn, who left it to his wife Cristiana for her lifetime, to pass to their son John when she died. After John sold it to John Randolf in 1328, it seems to have changed hands regularly, and at least nine times before being purchased by the gild in 1507. It did not stay long in the gild's possession either, and was later transferred to the ownership of the gild of Corpus Christi, where it remained until the gilds ceased to function.

The usual pattern of processions and activities was observed by the gild of St. Thomas. One specific rule was that all members were expected to attend the funeral services for their fellows, having placed two candles around the body. It was also decreed that on the feast of the translation of St. Thomas all members were to assemble at the third hour and solemnly bear a candle to their chapel, hear mass, offer ½d and say a psalter of the Blessed Virgin Mary. Their procession of 1549 has special significance in the history of Wymondham. Many people, other than gild members, had also gathered in the town, either for their own pilgrimage to Becket's chapel, or to visit the fair, and it was against this background that the events leading to the Kett Rebellion were played out. We cannot be certain that the requiem mass for gild members, with the offering of ½d per head on the following Monday, actually took place that year.

In 1537 Henry VIII, supporting the pro-reformation changes being made within the church, attempted to prevent the worship of saints by directing that the name of St. Thomas of Canterbury should be erased from all church missals. Gild members' reaction to this, in Wymondham as elsewhere in the country, was to continue calling themselves by the name of St. Thomas, but pretending that their dedication was to the apostle of that name, and no longer to St. Thomas of Canterbury.

A list of books donated to churchwardens Robert Seman, Henry Symonds, and Robert Connold by priest John Symonds in 1551, refers to an account book, "of the late guild of Beckettes begynnyng in the vi yere of Henry IV to the yere of our lord 1538". This suggests that in Wymondham the pretence of renaming did not last long, and that 1538 was the last year of the full operation of the gild. In the 1549-51 accounts, we read that the churchwardens were able to purchase a house and land which had belonged to the gild, with money obtained from merchant Thomas Cowper from the sale of lead, the income from which enabled them to pay the wages of the schoolmaster of the day.

The Gild of St. Peter

This must have been one of the most important and well-attended gilds in the town, although we have little detailed information of its activities. We do know, however, that Robert Ensyng was probably the last alderman, and that he had held certain sums of money from the gild of St. Peter after 1539. Some of these were paid to the churchwardens, and subsequently recorded in their accounts for the years 1549-1551. From taxation records, it appears that the gild had met as late as 1548.

In his history of Norfolk, Blomefield suggested that meetings were held at Suton, but there seems to be no additional evidence to support this theory. Blomefield's single reference, used for all subsequent studies of St. Peter's Gild, was "St. Peter of Sutton to which Aveline Bird gave 8 acres of land". Evidence from the wills does not support the view that the Gild of St. Peter met at Suton. It certainly owned land in that area, but so did other gilds. All the testators of the period definitely stated that their intention was to leave money to the Gild of St. Peter in Wymondham, although practically all those making bequests to the Holy Trinity specifically stated that that gild was in Spooner Row. Unfortunately we have been unable to locate the position of the gild hall or discover further documentation of the gild, and so the debate continues. Had the account book survived, it would probably have been a different story.

Further study of the wills reveal that the gild attracted many sizeable bequests. At a time when most did not exceed 3s 4d, some of these are particularly worthy of mention, for example those from three members, William Reve, Richard Glover, and vicar John Drye, were 6s 8d, while gifts of 10s by John Daundy and Robert Stalworth represent the largest bequests made to any single gild at this time. Taken together, this suggests that the Gild of St. Peter was certainly one of the most popular in Wymondham, with an higher than average membership, and that many of its members, such as Robert Hogon and Robert Ensyng, described as gentlemen, were from the more prosperous sections of the parish.

The extensive possessions of Gild of St. Peter are further indications of its wealth. However, some of these caused problems from time to time. In 1510 the brothers were brought to court and asked to show evidence of their right to hold certain copyhold messuages and lands in Wymondham. Robert Poynter, a chaplain, and also an alderman of the gild, was able to produce a document to this effect, but when a search was made of the manor rolls there was no reference to an entry of surrender. Thus Robert Poynter's document was declared a fake. Fortunately, he was an able and eloquent speaker, and at the subsequent court hearing confessed that his predecessors as alderman had been negligent. He quickly yielded up the lands to the lord of the manor, whose response was to allow the gild to keep them, as he wanted to continue the relief of the souls of the departed members of the gild and the continuation of the gild itself. In fact, altogether the alderman was granted one messuage, fifteen acres of land and a meadow, in diverse pieces, previously belonging to John Wetherby and a messuage and twenty acres of land, formerly in the possession of John Langforth. It was also allowed to keep a grove and piece of land without copy. The result of this generosity was that, in return, the gild was able to employ a parish priest to pray in accordance with the wishes of the lord of the manor. A review of the lands purchased by Sir Edward Clere in 1536, and later rented to Nicholas Dickenson, indicates that the gild of St. Peter also possessed land in Silfield

After the dissolution, some of these lands were purchased by the churchwardens, and we read of the rents collected by them in their accounts for the year 1549, as follows:-

3 acres in Northfield	3s
1 close in Smallcroft	11s
2 acres by Teddes field } 3 acres in Parkfield }	13 8d
3 closes	26s 8d
3 acres in Bondes field	2s
1 tenement	3s 8d
1 tenement	4s 4d
1 tenement	6s

It is interesting to note that the close in Smallcroft was rented by Robert Ensyng, the gild's last alderman, and the reference to the lands belonging to the "late" gild of St. Peter indicates that it had ceased to function at this date.

These lands eventually became part of the town lands, and in 1561 were surrendered to the Queen, together with a fine for rents due. All of them were subsequently returned to certain key officials of the town, and through them the whole parish, upon the condition that they take all the profits to pay for a schoolmaster in the town to educate boys. This, however, did not represent the first school to be established in the town. As we have seen, the churchwardens' accounts for the years 1544 to 1546 reveal payments being made for repairs to the schoolhouse, the setting up of stools there, and the wages of a schoolmaster. In 1550, the "heed skolemaster" was paid £4 for part of his annual stipend.

The Gild of the Holy Cross (Rood)

The old English meaning of 'rood' is 'cross', and in most medieval churches there would have been a decorative stone or wooden screen, separating the nave from the chancel and supporting a rood loft. Above this was the Great Rood, a carved and painted figure of the crucified Christ, usually flanked by the figures of the Blessed Virgin Mary and St. John. The rood in Wymondham Abbey was almost certainly mounted on the two medieval corbels, which still carry the Comper Rood. The difference in the clerestory windows suggests that the screen itself probably stood two bays west of where it stands today, separating the chancel, controlled by the monks, from the nave, which was the territory of the parish.

Many gilds in England and on the continent, named after the Holy Rood, claimed to have a relic of the original cross of Christ in their possession, and Wymondham was no exception. Slivers of the famous manger and the true cross, enclosed with other relics in a silver cross, were presented to Wymondham as a token of the seal of the grant of Happisburgh by William D'Albini, rather touchingly on the day of his wife's burial.

Our meagre documentation of the life of this gild reveals that the membership was not as high as some of those more popular at this time. There were only ten bequests recorded in the surviving wills, but these were of varied sums, with two of 3s 4d, perhaps indicating an average amount of wealth of the members. The individual sums are recorded below.

Bequests to the gild

1501	Katherine Metyngham	12d
1503	John Byshop	gift no sum given
1504	William Strowger	12d
1508	William Brown	20d
1515	Margaret Spylsby	20d
1520	Thomas Coke(Blexter)	20d
1520	William Fedymont	3s 4d
1520	William Payn	3s 4d
1522	Katherine Candeler	20d
1522	Agnes Davy	20d

References to property transactions are similarly scarce. The first surviving reference is a title deed for 1471, indicating its possession of a messuage in Wymondham, for which it paid an annual rent of 17½d, and which was still in gild ownership in 1494. That the gild owned other lands in the town is evident by a deed of 1534, in which some are conveyed to butcher Thomas Kett, alias Knyght, of Forncett, in 1534. This transacton required Kett to pay the gild the sum of £14 over the 40s already paid, prior to the finalisation of the deal, and an annual sum of 4d. Five years later, two further pieces of gild land, measuring on average 100 ft by 35 ft, and 66 ft by 20 ft, were transferred to the individual ownership of Francis Gedney. One of them joined the land which had already been sold to Thomas Kett in 1534. Thus we know that the gild, which had met within the manor of Norton, continued to operate until at least 1539.

The Gild of Saint George

Once again, our sources of information are very few, and we are limited to a very brief Latin transcription by Carthew of two years' accounts of the gild of St. George for 1532 and 1536, although he mistakenly dates the latter as 1436. We do have detailed records of the Gild of St. George in Norwich, and evidence suggests that its counterpart in Wymondham was organised in a similar way, if less grand. The Norwich gild had an aldermen, two masters and a council of twenty, but in Wymondham, the ruling body was just the alderman and the usual Election of twelve

An image of St. George in the church, maintained to the best of their ability by gild members, was the focal point for religious activities. Concern for the appearance of this resulted in bequests of 3s 4d being made in 1522 by both Agnes Davy and John Hendry in order that it could be repainted. It has been stated in a previous study that the gild of St. George met in Wattlefield. I have found no evidence to support this view in the bequests of the early sixteenth century, and indeed have checked very carefully the will of William Plomer, which is supposed to support the Wattlefield theory. It very definitely states that the gild of St. George was in Wymondham.

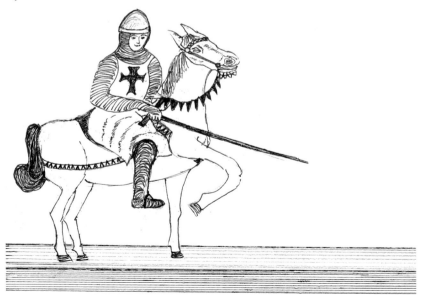

As to be expected, procession and pageantry were integral parts of the life of any gild dedicated to St. George, and this may well have been a deciding factor in the minds of people when they came to entering gilds for the first time. The first event on St. George's Day was a procession, of which St. George himself was naturally the central figure, always depicted on horseback, and usually attired in imitation armour. In Norwich, a man was selected and paid to represent him, while another accompanied him, walking inside the painted model of a dragon. Both were supposed to join in conflict throughout the procession.

In Wymondham, models may have been substituted for people. This would explain a Wymondham indenture of 1520, which describes the construction of a "ryding George", together with a dragon and an image of a horse fifteen hands high, being set up in the parish church. The original contract for this work, probably removed and not returned by Carthew, was between the parishioners and "William Bale graver of Wymondham and Thomas Sterlyng of Wymondham graver" and was dated 7th October 1519. This "rydyng George" was to be like the one at Lowestoft, except "the lyeng of the Dragon schall vary from the seid patron (pattern) for thys dragon schall lye rampyng on the seid

Figures of St. George and the dragon were set on a beam in the parish church in Wymondham.

beam". Another document, this time the accounts for the "Watch and Play Society" for 1538, refers to the purchase of canvas for a coat of armour, which may have been a replacement for the one usually borrowed for the St. George's Day festivities. However it was made, the horse would have been highly decorated with ribbons and laces, and attended by two henchmen, suitably attired. Further colour was added by the gild banner, borne aloft bearing the arms of St. George, the poorer members carrying candles, and the presence of the town waits in all their finery. In Norwich, it was compulsory for the brothers and sisters to provide and wear their own robes, which traditionally had to be red, but in Wymondham the procession would have been much more simple.

While researching in the library of the Norfolk and Norwich Archaeological Society, I discovered a hand-written single sheet of paper which was a transcription of a bill for a larger than usual feast, together with transcriptions of the 1532 and 1536 accounts for this gild in the same hand. On closer scrutiny, I found that the two years' accounts were the exact replicas of those appearing in the 1884 volume of Norfolk Archaeology, and they can therefore be attributed to Carthew. This leads me to believe that the list must also be his work and likewise refers to the gild of St. George in Wymondham. If so, it reveals how well the members fared on St. George's Day that year, and presumably other years. Purchases included 2 calves, 6 sheep, 7 pigs, 26 geese, 2 combs of wheat, 1 comb of malt, and 2 barrels of beer. Additional expenses for the carriage of wood, faggots, beer and tables, the grinding of the wheat, the hiring of pewter vessels, and the services of a cook and 2 dishwashers, completed the bill which totalled £3 15s 1½d. Unfortunately the receipts do not appear to have been enough to cover the expenses, although 24d was recouped from the sale of 2 sheepskins and 2 calves skins.

These vast quantities of meat eaten at such festive occasions may surprise us today, but it was often the only item on the menu, and the staple diet of the more wealthy. The lack of a balanced diet led to much suffering in all ranks of society, and modern theory suggests that the king himself was not immune. The open sores on his legs improved slightly during the months that fruit was available

An interesting find, in the records of the Gild of St. George in

Norwich, provides us with further information relating to the history of Wymondham. In 1485, a certain Thomas Drye was appointed feastmaker there, and following the usual process of gild appointments, rose to become a member of its ruling party three years later, a positon he held until 1506. Six years after this, John Drye, his son, became chaplain to the gild and was paid an annual salary of 8 marks or 6s 8d, for which he had to celebrate mass in the cathedral daily for the souls of the departed brethren and sisters of the gild. The following year, the same John moved to Wymondham, to become its vicar, and a member of its own gild of St. George. By 1532, he had become its alderman.

The gild's acquisition and letting of property seems to have followed the usual pattern, and Carthew's notes reveal that in 1532 Katherine Sleet paid 8s 8d for the rent of an enclosure and kitchen, Thomas Braskygge paid 3s for the rent of land, and Robert Kett and John Neve paid 12d for the rent of a dovecote, which they had been granted for twenty years, provided that they did not keep cattle on the surrounding land and that they paid their rent promptly on the gild day. No doubt there were several other properties.

Bequests to the gild

1508	William Brown	2s
1508	James Reynolds	2s
1510	Thomas Foster	20d
1520	William Fedymont	3s 4d
1522	Agnes Davy	3s 4d
1522	John Hendry (Spooner)	3s 4d
1525	William Reynolds sen	8d
1526	John Kensy sen	3s 4d
1528	Elizabeth Fox	6d
1533	Agnes Reynolds	6d
1535	William Plomer	8d

The Gild of Saint Margaret

A chapel on the north side of the church was dedicated to St. Margaret, but it was the property of the Abbey, and therefore could not be used by the parishoners. Evidence from the Bede Roll suggests that the Gild of St. Margaret held their devotions before a tabernacle in the Lady Chapel, dedicated to their patron saint, and which had been made and gilded by William Lombe. We know practically nothing about the activities of the gild which met there, but the wills available for the early sixteenth century reveal that thirteen members left bequests to the gild. Robert Chapelyn was a staunch supporter, which may have been the reason for the choice of the saint's name for his daughter. It is also interesting to note that the same Reynolds and Davy families and William Plomer, appearing in the list for the gild of St. George, are also included in this one.

Bequests to the gild

1500	Robert Chapelyn	3s 4d
1504	Thomas Kok	12d
1507	James Dawndy	3s 4d
1508	James Reynolds	2s
1513	Edmund Kytmay	3s 4d
1518	William Davy	20d
1518	Robert Stalworthe	12d
1518	Thomas Reynolds	12d
1519	John Reynolds	12d
1519	William Symonds	20d
1522	Agnes Davy	20d
1525	William Reynolds	4d
1526	John Kensy sen	3s 4d
1535	William Plomer	8d

The Gild of St. Laurence

Available evidence suggests that the Gild of St. Laurence was one of the smaller gilds in the town. In common with many of the others, however, it had a gilded tabernacle in the church as the focus for the religious activities of its members. A particular feature was its generosity to the parish church, even more remarkable in view of its comparative size. Not only did the members make a present of a cross and staff of copper and gilt, they also paid for the gilding of the seraphim at the high altar. In return for this generosity, the members of the Gild of St. Laurence were listed on the Bede Roll and prayed for regularly by the parishioners.

Bequests to the gild

1509	Emma Lynn	12d
1510	Thomas Foster	20d
1517	Nicholas Mekylfeld	16d
1518	Thomas Englyshe	20d

The Gild of Corpus Christi

Corpus Christi gilds were especially prominent in the fifteenth century. Pope Urban VI had founded the feast of Corpus Christi, the central feature of which was a solemn procession headed by the Blessed Sacrament. Corpus Christi gilds usually became wealthy, and this certainly seems to have been the case in Wymondham, where it acquired a wide-ranging collection of lands and properties. In fact these lands provide us with the only documentation for the gild, since there is not a single bequest or reference to it in the surviving wills. The list of books delivered by priest John Symonds to the churchwardens in 1551 includes 26 deeds of diverse lands belonging to the "late gild of Corpus Christi", together with 30 copies and one quittans concerning the copyhold of lands belonging to the gild.

Two title deeds confirm that it was operating at a later time than many of its contemporaries. One records a purchase in 1544 of a close of pasture and three roods of arable land in Northfield, near Ryealds Faldgate, and the second, made two years later in 1546, refers to an acre of pasture, surrounded on all sides by the common pasture of Wymondham, "now belonging to the gild of Corpus Christi". The use of the present tense in the latter verifies that it was still functioning at this time.

We also learn from the deeds the names of five members of the gild, and that this is another one of which the priest John Symonds was an alderman. He really was an outstanding personality in the town at this time, and an excellent example of a local man made good. The elder son of William Symonds, a fairly wealthy landowner, the title "sir" given to him in contemporary documents indicates that he was well educated and probably held a degree. He was a member of practically all the gilds for which we have records, the alderman of at least four of them, and the compiler of accounts for others. He also held a position of authority within the parish church, and was responsible for its collection of books and the costumes of the Watch and Play Society. His name also appears on countless wills made at this time, either as an executor or a witness. One gets the feeing that here was a man who was respected and trusted by the whole community.

Gilds in neighbouring parishes

We have seen that brothers and sisters from neighbouring parishes joined gilds in Wymondham. The traffic was not all in one direction, and in a reciprocal arrangement some Wymondham inhabitants travelled beyond the parish boundaries to join other gilds. The most popular of these was that of St. James in Crownthorpe, if we consider the number of bequests made in wills. Others which attracted donations from Wymondham members were those dedicated to St. Botolph in Morley, St. Andrew in Wicklewood, John the Baptist in Besthorpe, Our Lady in Carleton Forehoe, St. John in Mulbarton, All Saints in Tacolneston and St. Nicholas in Fundenhall. The majority of these gilds lie to the south and west of Wymondham, that is they are in the the same deanery, that of Hingham. Whether this was an important factor in influencing a choice of gild to join or whether it was more a matter of geography, we cannot be certain. Of the three outside this area, Robert Brown had perhaps lived in Tacolneston at one time, since we know that his brother John lived there at the time of Robert's death. The reason for Katherine Curtis leaving a bequest to the gild of St. John in Mulbarton, as well as to two Wymondham gilds, is less clear, although it may have been for a similar reason. John Dey certainly had family connections with parishes to the south-west of Wymondham, leaving bequests to the church at Ashwellthorpe, as well as to the Fundenhall gild.

Wymondham and its neighbouring parishes

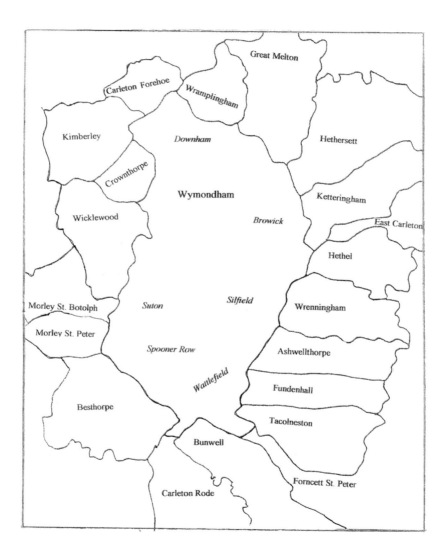

Wymondham members leaving bequests to gilds outside the parish

St. James in Crownthorpe	1501	Katherine Metyngham
	1502	John Caly
		William Dyman
	1503	Richard Metyngham
	1508	William Caly
	1520	William Fedymont
	1522	Agnes Davy
	1528	Isabella Fox
	1538	Rose Seman
St. Botolph, in Morley	1504	Thomas Kok
		John Colyour
		Alice Wodecok
St. Andrew in Wicklewood	1518	Thomas English
St. John the Baptist in Besthorpe	1522	Alice Wodecok
Our Lady in Carleton Forehoe	1505	Thomas Metyngham
	1530	John Lowe
St. John in Mulbarton	1503	Katherine Curtis
St. Nicholas in Fundenhall	1523	John Dey
All Saints in Tacolneston	1500	Robert Brown

The total number of eighteen represents approximately 11% of the 167 surviving Wymondham wills

Conclusion

The traditions and activities of the religious gilds of Wymondham had a profound effect upon the life of the town as a whole and on the members as individuals, which continued right up to their demise in the first part of the sixteenth century. I am convinced that the level of membership in the period under discussion was much larger than has previously been thought, and that most of the wealthy, and a high proportion of the less well-off, belonged to at least one gild, some to as many as six. We know that vicar John Drye belonged to at least eight. Although our records are limited, and available for less than half of the gilds functioning at this time, the analysis of those we do have is an interesting exercise. For the period 1500 until 1540, when many had ceased to operate, 86% of all testators living within the parish, whose wills have survived, were members of at least one gild. Of the remainder, 6% were widows, whose names suggest that their husbands were members, and in only 8% can I find no connection with a gild at all. These figures are all the more surprising when we remember that little or no documentation is available for seven of the twelve gilds, and that it was not necessarily the comparatively wealthy alone who made wills. The Church, certainly before the Reformation, taught that will-making was as much a duty as a right, and an expected part of the Christian's preparation for death.

Activities involving such a high proportion of the town cannot fail to have made some impact upon it. The close association between the gilds and the Abbey before dissolution, and between the gilds and the parish church before and after dissolution, undoubtedly increased the loyalty and devotion of gild members to those institutions. The Bede Roll of 1524 reveals that, of the many gifts made to the church during the fifteenth and early sixteenth century, four were made by individual gilds and more than half of them by individuals who were members of the gilds between 1500 and 1524. The maintenance of gild properties provided employment for local labour within the parish, and rarely was it necessary to call in experts from as far away as Norwich. Thus thatchers, masons, carpenters, carriers, wax chandlers, waits, and providers of food and drink, together with ordinary labourers, were all provided with work. Sometimes they belonged to the gild offering work, sometimes they did not.

The practice of gild members to request priests to say masses for their souls and their friends' souls after death meant that additional priests were employed in the parish, adding prestige and importance to the town. These "honest and secular priests" were required for various lengths of time, which usually depended upon the wealth of the gild member. For wealthy members like Robert Chapelyn it was possible to employ a priest for ten years, although the majority of requests were for a much shorter period.

What did the individual gain from gild membership? Certainly peace of mind, in the knowledge that his or her funeral expenses would be covered if there were insufficient funds in the personal estate, and that the prayers of many would petition for the rapid progression from purgatory to the heavenly realm. Gild stock, in the form of money or animals, offered members the opportunity to begin or expand a business enterprise, while office holding within the gild, usually beginning with the post of feastmaker, enabled many to develop what would have been otherwise their latent talents in this sphere. This may go some way to explain why, of the twelve churchwardens, recorded in the first three sets of the churchwardens' accounts between 1544 and 1553, five were men who had served on the ruling body of at least one gild, and three were the sons of gild officials. We must not over-generalise, however, since it would also be fair to say that these families belonged to the more prosperous section of the community and may well have been chosen in any case. Nevertheless, their previous experience of leadership would have been helpful. Community spirit was certainly engendered by the membership of gilds, and mutual help offered. The fact that members left bequests to so many, nine in the case of Agnes Davy, though not all in Wymondham, indicated they felt that belonging to such an organisation was well worth the comparatively few charges demanded of them.

Table of Gild Members

The following is a list of all the Wymondham inhabitants referred to in any document studied, with a record of the gilds to which they belonged, marked with a *. A double asterisk ** indicates that the member belonged to a gild described in his/her will as The Gild of St. Thomas in Wattlefield.

The symbol **B** is used to denote a bequest made by a member to the gild and the date at the end of the entry is the date of the bequest. **W** implies that the member worked for the gild in some capacity, including that of chaplain.

There is no column for the Gild of Corpus Christi because I had been unable to trace any members, but at the point of going to print, one or two were discovered. These have been marked with a **CC** in the column for the date of bequests.

Where it is known that a wife was also a member of the gild, but her name is not given, the husband's name is marked **+ wife**. Where any linkage is known, the husband's name is bracketed after the wife's entry.

Occupations are included if known.

	Virgin Mary	Lady's Light	John the Baptist	All Saints	Holy Trinity	Saint Thomas	Saint Peter	Saint Margaret	Saint Laurence	Saint George	Holy Cross	Date of bequest
Agas William	*											
Alden Richard	*			*								
Alen Agnes (John)			*									
Alen John			*									
Alexander Henry			*									
Angell Margaret	*			*								
Appilton Henry	*											
Appleyard Edmond	*											
Appleyard Margaret	*											
Appleyard William gent	*B											1503
Archerd Agnes widow				*								
Athos William priest	*											
August Brother monk				*								
Bacon Thomas	*											
Bale Isabella (John)	*	*	*									
Bale John	*	*	*									
Bale Robert	*	W	W									
Bale William	W	W	W	W		*B						1527
Ball Robert						*B						1528
Ballard William chaplain			*									
Banke John			*									
Banyard Edmund gent			*									
Bardwell Peter chaplain	*B											1518
Baxter John			*	*								
Baxter Richard	*											
Baxter Robert	*		*									
Bell Mawte	*											
Bell Thomas	W		*	*	*					*		
Belman Richard				*								
Belys Alys (Peter)	*		*									
Belys Peter	*		*									
Bery Robert		W										
Bery William monk			*	*								
Besom Thomas		*										
Beston William				W								
Bette John			*									
Betts Symond granor		W										
Bettes William smythe	*	W			W							
Blexter Agnes (Robert)			*									
Blexter Margaret			*									
Blexter Robert			*									
Blome Richard					*							
Blythe Jone (William)				*								
Blythe Symond	*											
Blythe Thomas				*								
Blythe William				*								
Bokenham Thomas		*										
Borrell Richard		W										
Borrell Stephen	*	*					*					
Borrell Thomas	*B											1506
Borrow John wax chandler		W				**B						1523
Borrow William		W										
Bote Richard	*					*B						1504
Boteler Cateryn				*B								1501
Bradforth Laurence	*+wife											

	Virgin Mary	Lady's Light	John the Baptist	All Saints	Holy Trinity	Saint Thomas	Saint Peter	Saint Margaret	Saint Laurence	Saint George	Holy Cross	Date of bequest
Bradforth Robert					*	*B						1508
Bradyr John	*											
Branforth John (ABBOT)	*											
Breeze Agnes				*B								1501
Brice Beatrice (John)			*									
Brice John			*									
Bristow Marion (Robert)			*									
Bristow Robert			*B									1530
Brome Richard		*										
Brome Robert		*										
Bromefort Robert					*							
Bron John			*									
Bron Richard	*											
Bron Thomas			*									
Brondale William			*									
Brother Isabel	*											
Brother John		*	*									
Brown Harry	*W	*		*								
Brown Jeorge					*B							1527
Brown John ??					*							
Brown Richard					*						*	
Brown Robert					*B		*B					1500
Brown Stephen					*							
Brown Thomas of Morley					*							
Brown William	*B				*B	*B				*B	*B	1508
Buk William priest	*											
Bunne Peter					*							
Burgess Matilda(William)		*B	*									1530
Burgess Nicolas										*		
Burgess Roger		*B										1530
Burgess William	*	*	*									
Burne John of Besthorpe					*							
Bylaw John mason		W										
Bylawe Margaret (Thomas)			*									
Bylawe Thomas wait												
Byrd Walter		*										
Byshopp Adam priest	*	*						*				
Byshopp John	*	*									*B	1503
Caly Agnes		*										
Caly Alice(William jun)			*									
Caly Isabella(William sen)			*									
Caly Joanna (John)			*									
Caly John the elder d1502			*B			*B						1502
Caly John			*									
Caly Margaret(Robert)		*										
Caly Margaret(Richard)			*									
Caly Richard	*		*									
Caly Robert	*	*		*B								1511
Caly Thomas			*B									1542
Caly William sen	*		*B			*B						1509
Caly William jun	*		*B									1530
Candeler Katherine						*B					*B	1522
Candeler Thomas	*											
Carne Robert			*+ wife									
Carne William		*										

104

Wymondham Gild Members

	Virgin Mary	Lady's Light	John the Baptist	All Saints	Holy Trinity	Saint Thomas	Saint Peter	Saint Margaret	Saint Laurence	Saint George	Holy Cross	Date of bequest
Caron Richard				*								
Carre Alice(John)			*									
Carre John			*W									
Carr Margaret(Thomas)		*										
Carr Richard					*							
Carr Robert		*	*+wife		*					*		
Carr Thomas		*										
Carrow Joan	*											
Carrow Thomas bailie	*		*	*			*					
Carter William(Carlet. Rod	*+ wife											
Castleton William			*+wife									
Cayster Robert priest		*										
Challey Matilda				*								
Chambers John				W								
Chantrell Elizabeth widow	*											
Chapleyn Christian(Robert	*											
Chapleyn Margaret	*											
Chapleyn Robert	*B				*B	*B		*B				1500
Chapleyn William	*											
Chapman Thomas	*											
Cheeseman Agnes(Thomas	*		*									
Cheeseman John				*								
Cheeseman Thomas	*	*	*									
Chetryng Thomas	* +wife	*										
Churche Isabella (Thomas)			*							*		
Churche Thomas			*									
Clerke Alice				*								
Clerke John			*									
Clerke Robert				*								
Clerke William			*									
Cok John			*									
Coke Agnes					*							
Coke John	W	W										
Coke Robert				W								
Coke Thomas (Blexter)	*	*				*B					*B	1520
Coke William		*										
Coly Margaret		*										
Colman John sen					*							
Colman John jun					*							
Colman Richard jun					*							
Colman Robert sen					*							
Colman Robert jun					*							
Colman Thomas sen					*							
Colman Thomas jun					*							
Colton Peter					*							
Colyour Ames		W										
Colyour James	*				*							
Colyour John d 1519	*B	*	*	*B	*B							1519
Colyour John d 1534	*B	*	*B		*							1534
Colyour Katherine				*								
Colyour Richard	*	*			*							
Colyour Thomas			*		*							
Connell John priest			*									
Cook Agnes		*										
Cook Catherine (Thomas)			*									
Cook Thomas			*			*				*		

	Virgin Mary	Lady's Light	John the Baptist	All Saints	Holy Trinity	Saint Thomas	Saint Peter	Saint Margaret	Saint Laurence	Saint George	Holy Cross	Date of bequest
Cote John				*								
Coper Francis + wife				*								
Cornwell Edmund	W	*										
Cornwell Thomas		*										
Cotyngham Agnes		*B	*B									1538
Cotyngham John				*								
Cowper Robert	W											
Cowper Thomas	*						*					
Cowper William	W											
Crane William			*									
Crashfeld Robert	W			*	*							
Creak John				*								
Curson Edmundof Kimberley			*									
Curson James (monk)				*								
Curson Johanna				*								
Curson John				*								
Curson Margaret(John)				*								
Curtis Katherine	*B						*B					1503
Cuschen Agnes				*								
Cuschen John				*								
Dalys James priest				*								
Dalys Thomas priest	*B		*B		*B							1510
Dan Robert		*										
Davy Agnes	*B		*B				*B	*B		*B	*B	1522
Davy Joanna	*											
Davy John	*			*			*					
Davy Brother				*								
Davy William	*B						*B					1518
Daundy John	*+wifeB						*B	*B				1507
Daynes Richard							*B					1522
Dekyn Thomas					*							
Denton Margaret(Richard)				*								
Denton Richard	*			*								
Deplage Robert				*								
Dewe John				*								
Dey John							*B					1523
Dey Robert	W	*	W	W	W							
Dey Thomas							*B					1515
Dey William				*			*					
Deynes Alice (Richard)			*	*								
Deynes Isabel		*		*								
Deynes John				*								
Deynes Richard spooner			*	*	*							
Dixon John	*											
Dobbys Robert		*										
Dobbys Thomas	*			*								
Donnyng John					*							
Donthorne John				*								
Dowe Katherine(William)				*	*							
Dowe Peter				*	*							
Dowe William				*B	*							1522
Dowglas Robert		*										
Dowsyng Thomas				*								
Dowsyng William	*				*							
Drake Robert		*		*								

	Virgin Mary	Lady's Light	John the Baptist	All Saints	Holy Trinity	Saint Thomas	Saint Peter	Saint Margaret	Saint Laurence	Saint George	Holy Cross	Date of bequest
Drye John (Vicar)	*B	*B	*	*	*	*B	*B			*		1537
Dunthorne John + wife				*								
Dyman Alice (Richard)	*											
Dyman Henry	* +wife	*		*								
Dyman Richard	*	*										
Dyman William				*B								1502
Dynes Thomas				*								
Dyn John	*	*		*	*					*		
Dyn Robert	*+ wife	*	*		*					*		
Dynne Margaret				*								
Dynnys Philip	*											
Dynnys Thomas	*											
Elyett Robert		*+wife			*+wife							
Elyngham Thomas				*+wife								
Englyshe Richard	*W	W	W	W								
Englyshe Thomas									*B			1518
Ensyng Robert gent	* +wife						*					
Esmond Thomas monk				*								
Fauce Margaret(Thomas)			*									
Fauce Thomas	*		*B									1539
Fedymont Edward					*B							1500
Fedymont(Potter) Isabella			*		*							
Fedymont Joanna (John 1)			*									
Fedymont John 1			*	*								
Fedymont John 2					*							
Fedymont Margaret (John 2)					*							
Fedymont Richard			*	*						*		
Fedymont Thomas					*							
Fedymont William				*B			*B			*B	*B	1520
Fischpond John	*											
Flory Robert					W							
Flowerdew David monk				*								
Flowerdew John	* +wife											CC
Flowerdew Katherine (Will	*											
Flowerdew William	*											
Flye Joanna (John)	*											
Flye John	*											
Ford Robert + wife				*								
Fordham John			*		*							
Fordham Margaret (John)					*							
Fordham Robert		W	*	*								
Fosse Henry			*									
Foster John	W			W								
Foster Rose widow				*								
Foster Thomas d1510			*	*	*B				*B	*B		1510
Foster Thomas d1516				*B								1516
Foster William		*		W						*		
Foteman John				*								
Fowler Henry			W									
Fox Agnes (John)	*											
Fox Isabella	*B		*B			*B				*B		1528
Fox John	*											
Fox Richard			*				*					
Fraunces Jone		*		*B								1527

107

	Virgin Mary	Lady's Light	John the Baptist	All Saints	Holy Trinity	Saint Thomas	Saint Peter	Saint Margaret	Saint Laurence	Saint George	Holy Cross	Date of bequest
Freeman Robert				*								
Frewell Helen (John)			*									
Frewell John			*									
Frosdyk Agnes (William)			*									
Frosdyk James	*B	*B	*	*B								1528
Frosdyk Joanna	*			*								
Frosdyk Robert priest	*			*								
Frosdyk William d1518		*B	*B									1518
Frosdyk William			*+wife									
Fryer Matthew				*								
Fuller Edmond					*							
Fynke Joanna (John)			*									
Fynke John			*									
Fyshpond John + wife				*								
Galle Alice (John)				*								
Galle Isabel				W								
Galle John		*		*W								
Galyon Gregory +wife				*								
Garnett John + wife				*								
Garrard William				*								
Gay Agnes (Geoffrey)		*										
Gay Elizabeth		*										
Gay Geoffrey		*										
Gay John		*		*								
Gay William		*						*B				1507
Gedney Francis		*										
Glover Edmond				*								
Glover Richard	*B							*B				1504
Godfrey John mason				*								
Godfrey John glover				*								
Godfrey Robert				*								
Godfrey Thomas				*B								1519
Gonned John priest	*											
Gorham John	*											
Grene Richard			*									
Grene Thomas			*									
Gresham Thomas monk				*								
Griffyn John	*											
Gronde Robert			*									
Grondger John				W								
Grower Margaret						*	*B					1509
Gummeld John			*									
Gybson Richard			*									
Gylden Richard			*									
Gylden Robert			*									
Gylforth Robert	*		*									
Halle Richard			*									
Hammond Edmund	*	*										
Hammond John		*										
Hamont Batholomew			*									
Hamont John	W	*			W							
Hamont Richard					W							
Hamont William	*W											
Harecroft John			*									

	Virgin Mary	Lady's Light	John the Baptist	All Saints	Holy Trinity	Saint Thomas	Saint Peter	Saint Margaret	Saint Laurence	Saint George	Holy Cross	Date of bequest
Harecroft Thomas			*									
Harecroft William			*									
Harrald John	*	*		W								
Harrald Margaret (John)	*											
Harvy Alice (John)			*									
Harvy John			*									
Harvy Stephen			*									
Hed Elise	*											
Hed John	*	*										
Hed Olyva	*											
Hemlyn Reynald		*										
Hempsale Thomas			W	W	W							
Hendry Isabella (Thomas)			*	*								
Hendry al Spooner John		*B	*B							*B		1522
Hendry Robert		*										
Hendry al Spooner Thomas		*	*	*+wives					*			
Hengham John monk				*								
Heynes John			W	W								
Hobbes Agnes (John)			*									
Hobbes Elizabeth (Thomas)			*									
Hobbes John			*+wife									
Hobbes Robert			*									
Hobbes Thomas			*B			*B						1535
Hodson Agnes (William)			*									
Hodson William			*		*							
Hogges John			*									
Hogon Catherine (Nicholas)			*									
Hogon Nicholas			*			*B						1533
Hogon Robert gent							*					
Hogon Thomas			*									
Hood Agnes			*									
Horby Catherine (Stephen)			*									
Horby Stephen			*									
Horncrek William monk				*								
Howse Batholomew			*									
Howse Margaret (Richard)			*	*								
Howse Richard of Besthorpe			*	*	*							
Howse Robert					*							
Howse Sybyl (Batholomew)			*									
Hurrye Thomas				*						*		
Hylle Ames		*										
Hylle Isabel				*								
Hyll William		*										
Hynde Margaret				*								
Ilward Richard		W										
Ilward Thomas		W										
Irby Robert Vicar	*	*	*	*								
Irby William schoolmaster	*											
Irenhed Richard	*	*										
Irenhed William	*											
Jeffrey Alexander					*							
Jeffrey Margaret (Thomas)				*								
Jeffrey Robert wait				*	*							
Jeffrey Thomas				*	*							

Wymondham Gild Members

	Virgin Mary	Lady's Light	John the Baptist	All Saints	Holy Trinity	Saint Thomas	Saint Peter	Saint Margaret	Saint Laurence	Saint George	Holy Cross	Date of bequest
Lombe Rosa	*											
Lombe Thomas gent	* +wife				*							
Lombe Thomas jun					*							
Lombe William gent	*											CC
Lovyk Alice (John)	*											
Lovyk John	*			*								
Lowes Agnes (Thomas)				*								
Lowes Thomas				*								
Luce Alice (Thomas sen)	*											
Luce Thomas sen	*				*							
Luce Thomas jun	*				*							
Lynn Emma widow									*B			1509
Lytylbery Rychard		*										
Lytyll Agnes (1 John sen)			*									
Lytyll Catherine (2 John sen)			*									
Lytyll John sen			*									
Lytyll John jun			*									
Lytyll Stephen			*									
Machyn Agnes (John)				*								
Machyn John				*								
Male George			W									
Male John	*	*										
Male Richard	*											
Malenger William			W									
Mannyng Joanna (John)			*									
Mannyng John smythe	*		*	W						*		
Mannyng John tailor	*											
Mannyng Margaret (Robert)	*	*	*									
Mannyng Robert						**B						1509
Mannyng Robert sen		*B	*B			**B						1512
Mannyng Simon			*B	*B	*B	**B						1505
Marchall Agnes (Edmund)				*								
Marchall Edmund				*								
Marrow John			*	W						*		
Marsham Agnes (Thomas)				*								
Marsham Thomas				*								
Martyn Agnes widow		*B						*B				1499
Martyn Cecilye (Richard)				*								
Martyn Henry	*				*							
Martyn Isabella (Henry)	*											
Martyn John					*							
Martyn Richard				*	*							
Martyn Thomas	*	*										
Mason Thomas				*								
Maste John	*											
Mayde Richard			*									
Mayde Ames		*										
Mayden John shopkeeper		*B						*B				1518
Mayden Robert		*										
Mayles Richard	*			*								
Mayour John	*W											
Mays John	*											
Mechel John	*	*		*								
Mechel Robert shoemaker		*										
Medylton John			*		*							

110

Wymondham Gild Members

	Virgin Mary	Lady's Light	John the Baptist	All Saints	Holy Trinity	Saint Thomas	Saint Peter	Saint Margaret	Saint Laurence	Saint George	Holy Cross	Date of bequest
Hobson John		*										
Toby Joanna (John sen)			*									
Toby Joanna (William			*									
Toby John sen		*	*									
Toby John jun		*	*	W								
Toby Katherine (John jun)			*									
Toby William			*									
Johnson Francis				*								
Jordan John			*B									1511
Just William			W									
Kebit John priest	*B						*B					1504
Kedell Maryon (Richard)				*								
Kedell Richard		*		*								
Kedell Thomas				*								
Kedell William	W									*		
Kellyngworth Josiah	* + wife											
Kempley Robert	*											
Kensy A		*										
Kensy Joanna (John jun)				*								
Kensy John sen	*B	*					*B	*B		*B		1526
Kensy John jun	*	*	*	*								
Kensy Robert	*	*					*					
Kersey John		*	*									
Kett(Knyght) John d1512		*			*	*B						1512
Kett(Knyght) John d1534		*	*	*	*							
Kett Nicholas			*									
Kett (Knyght) Robert		*										
Kett Thomas senior	* + wife		*		*					*		
Kett William		*		W			*					
Killyngworth Josiah	*											
Kirby Andrew		*		*								
Kirby Richard			*									
Knyght William		*										
Kok Thomas	*B				*B	**B		*B				1504
Kyng Amos		*										
Kyng Agnes (William 1)		*B		*B			*B					1526
Kyng Henry DD Vicar			*									
Kyng Margaret (William 2)				*								
Kyng William 1		*		*B								1517
Kyng William 2				*								
Kyrtelyng John Abbot			*									
Kytmay Alice				*								
Kytmay Amelia (Edmund)	*											
Kytmay Edmund	*B					*B		*B				1513
Langford John			*									
Laws Thomas	*											
Lawys John			*									
Lawys Margaret (John)			*									
Legett Joanna (John)			*									
Legett John			*									
Levald Margaret (William)				*B			*B					1528
Levald William		*		*			*					
Leveriche Hewe				*								

	Virgin Mary	Lady's Light	John the Baptist	All Saints	Holy Trinity	Saint Thomas	Saint Peter	Saint Margaret	Saint Laurence	Saint George	Holy Cross	Date of bequest
Lombe Rosa	*											
Lombe Thomas gent	* +wife				*							
Lombe Thomas jun					*							
Lombe William gent	*											CC
Lovyk Alice (John)	*											
Lovyk John	*			*								
Lowes Agnes (Thomas)				*								
Lowes Thomas				*								
Luce Alice (Thomas sen)	*											
Luce Thomas sen	*				*							
Luce Thomas jun	*				*							
Lynn Emma widow									*B			1509
Lytylbery Rychard		*										
Lytyll Agnes (1 John sen)			*									
Lytyll Catherine (2 John sen)			*									
Lytyll John sen			*									
Lytyll John jun			*									
Lytyll Stephen			*									
Machyn Agnes (John)				*								
Machyn John				*								
Male George				W								
Male John	*	*										
Male Richard	*											
Malenger William			W									
Mannyng Joanna (John)			*									
Mannyng John smythe	*		*	W						*		
Mannyng John tailor	*											
Mannyng Margaret (Robert)	*	*	*									
Mannyng Robert						**B						1509
Mannyng Robert sen		*B	*B			**B						1512
Mannyng Simon				*B	*B	**B						1505
Marchall Agnes (Edmund)				*								
Marchall Edmund				*								
Marrow John			*	W						*		
Marsham Agnes (Thomas)			*									
Marsham Thomas			*									
Martyn Agnes widow		*B						*B				1499
Martyn Cecilye (Richard)				*								
Martyn Henry	*				*							
Martyn Isabella (Henry)	*											
Martyn John					*							
Martyn Richard				*	*							
Martyn Thomas	*	*										
Mason Thomas				*								
Maste John	*											
Mayde Richard			*									
Mayde Ames		*										
Mayden John shopkeeper		*B						*B				1518
Mayden Robert		*										
Mayles Richard	*			*								
Mayour John	*W											
Mays John	*											
Mechel John	*	*		*								
Mechel Robert shoemaker		*										
Medylton John			*		*							

111

	Virgin Mary	Lady's Light	John the Baptist	All Saints	Holy Trinity	Saint Thomas	Saint Peter	Saint Margaret	Saint Laurence	Saint George	Holy Cross	Date of bequest
Medylton Margaret (John)			*									
Mekylfeld Alys	*B	*B										1505
Mekylfeld John	* +wife		*									
Mekylfeld Nicholas	*B						*B		*B			1517
Mekylfeld William baker	*+ wife										*	
Metyngham Alys (Richard)			*									
Metyngham James			*									
Metyngham John			*B	*								1538
Metyngham Katherine			*B			*B					*B	1501
Metyngham Richard			*B				*B					1503
Metyngham Richard			*B									1512
Metyngham Thomas		*B	*B		*B							1505
Monday John			*									
More Henry					*							
More John					*							
More Robert					*							
More Thomas					*							
More William		*										
Mortymer Joanna(Thomas)	*		*									
Mortymer Thomas	*+wife	W	*									
Multon Cecily (Harry)		*										
Multon Harry		*		*								
Munke John			*									
Myddilton Agnes (John)			*									
Myddilton John			*B				*B					1526
Mylsent Alexander			*									
Nele William				W								
Nelyng Katherine						*B						1528
Nelyng Robert priest	*	*BW										1523
Neve John		*								*		
New Peter			W									
Newlande Agnes(William)				*								
Newlande William	*			*								
Newman of Thorpe				W								
Newman Harry				W								
Newman John			W									
Newman Margaret (Robert)				*								
Newman Robert			*B			*B						1508
Newson William	*+ wife											
Newton Elizabeth widow			*									
Newton Isabella (Roland)			*									
Newton Roland			*									
Noryche George			W									
Offycyall Thomas			*									
Okdeyn Thomas priest			*									
Olyff Agnes (John)	*	W										
Olyff John	*B											1512
Pakk William Rector of Morley					*							
Palmer Robert						*B						1504
Parker Thomas				W								
Paristhe Richard				W								
Payn John			*	W								
Payn Isabella				*								

112

Wymondham Gild Members

	Virgin Mary	Lady's Light	John the Baptist	All Saints	Holy Trinity	Saint Thomas	Saint Peter	Saint Margaret	Saint Laurence	Saint George	Holy Cross	Date of bequest
Payn Letitia (Richard)			*	*								
Payn Richard		*	*	*								
Payn (Halle) William				*B		*B	*B				*B	1520
Paynter John		*										
Perle William		*		* + wife								
Perlyng John		*										
Perse John			W	W	W							
Petyt Christina (John)			*									
Petyt James				*								
Petyt John			*							*		
Petyt Margaret (James)				*								
Petyt Margaret (Thomas)		*		*								
Petyt Thomas		*		*								
Peynter James				*								
Peynter Johanna (James)				*								
Peynter William					*							
Platemaker Margaret (Richard)		*										
Platemaker Richard		*										
Platemaker Robert		*										
Platemaker Stephen		*										
Platemaker Thomas		*										
Plokett Richard		*										
Plomer Catherine (William)		*										
Plomer John		*		*								
Plomer Katherine	*B											1506
Plomer Richard		*										
Plomer Robert				*								
Plomer Thomas priest	*											
Plomer William		*B	*B			*B		*B		*B		1535
Polls John		*				**B						1501
Ponyant Elizabeth widow				*								
Porter Thomas vicar	*		*	*								
Potter John of Besthorpe					*							
Potter Richard	*		*	*	*							
Potter Robert				W								
Potter Stephen					*							
Poynter James		*										
Poynter Robert							*					
Pulham Isabel	*											
Pycher Laurence				W								
Pye John					*							
Pylett John				W								
Pynchon John priest	*				W							
Pynnar Richard			*									
Pynner Andrew wait				W	W							
Quentrell Elizabeth			*									
Quentrell Thomas smyth			*W									
Randoll John	*			*	*							
Randolf Roger priest	*											
Redmayn John Abbot	*											
Render Thomas		*										
Reve William priest d1518	*B											1518
Reve William		*	*									
Reynberd John			*									

113

	Virgin Mary	Lady's Light	John the Baptist	All Saints	Holy Trinity	Saint Thomas	Saint Peter	Saint Margaret	Saint Laurence	Saint George	Holy Cross	Date of bequest
Reynberd Margery (John)			*									
Reynolds Agnes (William)										*B		1533
Reynold Alys (Thomas)	*	*										
Reynold Catherine		*B										1521
Reynolds James					*B	*B		*B		*B		1508
Reynold John			*		*B	*B				*B		1519
Reynold Richard	*		*									
Reynold Thomas	*B	*				*B		*B				1518
Reynolds William	*				*B	*B		*B		*B		1525
Role Margaret			*									
Roo Robert				*								
Rome Geoffrey	*									*		
Rose Richard	W											
Rowchester John			*									
Rowchester William	*+wife											
Rowse Joanna (William 1)				*								
Rowse Lydya (William 2)				*								
Rowse Richard	*	*										
Rowse William				*								
Rudd John			*									
Russell Thomas				*								
Rynge John				*								
Rynger Robert monk				*								
Ryngwood Symond		*B						*B				1525
Ryngwood William			*	*								
Sallet Agnes (Simon)				*								
Sallet Simon				*								
Sawer John				*								
Sawer Margaret (John)				*								
Sawerd John				*								
Sawerd Symond		*		*								
Schere Nicolas		W										
Scott Adam		*										
Seker John				W								
Seman Agnes (Harry)				*								
Seman Harry	*W	W		*W								
Seman Richard				*								
Seman Robert	*											
Seman Rose	*B	*B										1538
Seman Thomas				*								
Seman Stephen	*B							*B				1515
Sendell Sybil (Thomas)				*								
Sendell Thomas		*W		*W								
Sewald William		*										
Seyns John			*									
Shere William	*B											1523
Shergate John					*+wife							
Sherperd John									*			
Simond John		*										
Skere John			*									
Skinner John				*								
Sme Richard			*									
Smyth James		*										
Smyth John		W	W	W								
Smythe Richard			*									

	Virgin Mary	Lady's Light	John the Baptist	All Saints	Holy Trinity	Saint Thomas	Saint Peter	Saint Margaret	Saint Laurence	Saint George	Holy Cross	Date of bequest
Smyth(alias Folsham)Robert			*									
Smythe WilliamWicklewod	*	*		*+wife	*B		*B					1528
Smythe Will.Wrenningham	*B											1523
Sothewell Francis	*											
Spyllysby Margaret	*B					*B					*B	1515
Stalworthe John			*									
Stalworthe Robert		W					*B	*B				1518
Stanton Petyr				*+wife								
Sterlyng Alyce(Robert)		W										
Sterlyng John		*										
Sterlyng Robert	*	*W	W									
Sterlyng Thomas	* +wife	W	W	W	W							
Sterlyng William			W									
Stephynson Margaret				*								
Stevynson Catherine (William)			*									
Stevynson William			*									
Stevyns William			*									
Stewman Henry	*											
Stokton Alice (Robert)			*									
Stokton Nicolas	* +wife	*	W									
Stokton Robert	* +wife		*									
Stokton William			*				*					
Ston Isabella (John)			*									
Ston John			*									
Strowger William											*B	1504
Sturman Geoffrey			*+wife									
Sturman Lucy			*									
Swete John				*								
Swetyng Henry		W										
Sygar Christian							*					
Sygar John priest d 1529				*B								1529
Sygar John the elder		*W			*						*	
Symonds Anna (Geoffrey 2)			*									
Symonds Edward	W	*		W								
Symonds Elizabeth (Roger)			*									
Symonds Geoffrey			*									
Symonds Henry	* +wife	*	W									
Symonds John priest	*	*W	*W									
Symonds John		*	*		*							
Symonds Margaret (John)			*									
Symonds Margaret(Geoffrey1)			*									
Symonds Robert	*	*		W		*B						1526
Symonds Roger			*									
Symonds William	*B			W		*B		*B				1519
Tedde Henry			*									
Thomas the mason		W										
Tetyssalle Alice (William)	*	*		*								
Tetyssalle John												CC
Tetyssalle William	*	*	*									
Todde Richard			W	W								
Toly Isabella (Robert)	*											
Toly Robert	*											
Toly Symond		*+wife										
Tornor A		*										
Tornor Thomas		W		W								

Wymondham Gild Members

	Virgin Mary	Lady's Light	John the Baptist	All Saints	Holy Trinity	Saint Thomas	Saint Peter	Saint Margaret	Saint Laurence	Saint George	Holy Cross	Date of bequest
Tryman Katherine				W								
Tye John		*		*+wife								
Tyler William				W								
Tyndchyte John				*								
Utting Thomas			*									
Vaunce Robert			*									
Vekere Robert	*+wife	*	W	W								
Verdon Margaret (Stephen)					*							
Verdon Stephen	*	*		*	*							
Vikyn Stephen			*+wife									
Vyntner Katherine	*											
Wacy John			*									
Walter John		*+ wife	*									
Walter Thomas		*	*									
Walter William	*+wife											
Waschyngton Thomas	*											
Warden Thomas			*B									1513
Warne John					*							
Watkyn Robert		*	*									
Wek Margaret				*								
Wende Thomas	*	*		*								
Wenlok Thomas			*									
Wetyn Robert			*									
Wetyng James		*										
Whitlawe Thomas			*									
Whytechyrche John				*								
Wode Thomas			*									
Wodecok Agnes (Robert)					*							
Wodecok Alyce (Richard?)			W		*B		*B					1522
Wodecok John	*				*							
Wodecok John junior					*							
Wodecok Richard					*B							1505
Wodecok Robert					*							
Wodecok Roger sawyer		W										
Wodecok Stephen					*							
Wodecok William Besthorpe					*							
Wodecok William junior					*							
Woodward Isabella (Robert)	*		*									
Woodward Robert			*									
Wryght Richard				*								
Wulterton Agnes	*B	*B	*B			*B	*B					1518
Wurlyngton Edmund			*									
Wurlyngton Johanna (William?)			*									
Wurlyngton William	*	*	*	W								
Wyllyngton Clemont	*	*										
Wyllyngton Margaret (Clem)	*	*										
Wylson Robert					*							
Wyndhows Robert monk				*								
Wynter Alice (William)			*									
Wynter William			*									
Wyseman Christina (Robert jun)			*	*								
Wyseman Robert	* +wife		*	*						*		
Wyseman William	*+wife			*	*							

Wymondham Gild Members

	Virgin Mary	Lady's Light	John the Baptist	All Saints	Holy Trinity	Saint Thomas	Saint Peter	Saint Margaret	Saint Laurence	Saint George	Holy Cross	Date of bequest
Wyseman William junior	*+wife											
Wytred Geoffrey					*							
Yole Margaret (Robert)			*									
Yole Robert			*									
Youngman Thomas	*	*								*		

117

BIBLIOGRAPHY

MANUSCRIPTS

(Transcriptions by author unless stated)

Wymondham Parish Records
Held in the Muniment Room, Wymondham Abbey

The Account Book of the Gild of the Nativity of the Blessed Virgin 1458-1544 WPR(10/1/1)

The Account Book of the Gild of St. John the Baptist 1504-1544 WPR (10/1/4)

The Account Book of the Gild of All Saints 1501-1536 WPR (10/1/3)

The Account Book of the Gild of the Holy Trinity 1517-1544 WPR (10/1/5)

The Account Book of the Gild of Our Lady's Light 1506-1527, 1536-1539 WPR (10/1/2)

The Churchwardens' Accounts 1544-1561 WPR (7/1)

The Wymondham Bede Roll 1524, (WPR 3/2/3) transcribed by Paul Cattermole WPR (Class II)

Title Deeds 1225-1546, calendered by Paul Cattermole

'The total of certain books, endentures and others delivered by John Symonds, priest to…..churchwardens, the 4th day of February, the fifth year of the reign of Edward Vl….' WPR (3/1/2)

Norfolk Record Office

167 wills 1500-1543 proved in the Norfolk Archdeaconry Court or the Norwich Consistory Court

View of the lands of Nicholas Dickenson   NRS 19422

PRIMARY PRINTED SOURCES and ARTICLES

P. Basing (ed.), *Parish Fraternity Register* (London Record Society, 1982)

G. A. Carthew, 'Extracts from papers in the Church Chest of Wymondham', in *Norfolk Archaeology* Volume 9 (1884)

G. A. Carthew, 'Wymondham Gilds', in *Norfolk Archaeology* Volume 9 (1884)

C. Firth, 'Village Gilds of Norfolk in the fifteenth century'. In *Norfolk Archaeology* Volume 18 (1914)

M. Grace (ed), *Records of the Gild of St. George in Norwich, 1389-1547*, Norfolk Record Society 9 (1937)

H. L. Haywood, 'Freemasonry and the guild system', in *The Builder* (November 1923)

S. Martin Jones, *Wymondham and its abbey*, Wymondham (1914)

J. F. Williams, 'The Gild of St. John the Baptist at Swaffham', in *Norfolk Archaeology* Volume 33 (1962-5)

BOOKS

F. Blomefield, *An Essay Towards a Topographical History of the County of Norfolk, Volume 2* (London 1805)

K. Farnhill, *Religious gilds and the parish community in late medieval East Anglia. C. 1470-1550,* (York 2001)

S. Friar, *The Local History Companion* (Stroud 2001)

R. Houlbrooke, *Death, Religion and the Family in England 1450-1750* (Oxford 1998)

C. Platt, *The Parish Churches of Medieval England* (London 1981)

P. Wade-Martins (ed), *An Historical Atlas of Norfolk* (Norwich 1993)

H. F. Westlake, *The Parish Gilds of Medieval England* (London, 1919)

INDEX FOR TEXT